FIERCE

Female Athletes Fueled by Faith

DEL DUDUIT & CARIS SNIDER

Birmingham, Alabama

Fierce

Iron Stream
An imprint of Iron Stream Media
100 Missionary Ridge
Birmingham, AL 35242
IronStreamMedia.com

Copyright © 2025 by Del Duduit and Caris Snider

No part of this publication may be reproduced, stored in a retrieval system, or transmitted in any form or by any means—electronic, mechanical, photocopying, recording, or otherwise—without the prior written permission of the publisher.

Iron Stream Media serves its authors as they express their views, which may not express the views of the publisher.

Library of Congress Control Number: 2025932911

Scripture quotations are from the ESV® Bible (The Holy Bible, English Standard Version®), © 2001 by Crossway, a publishing ministry of Good News Publishers. Used by permission. All rights reserved. The ESV text may not be quoted in any publication made available to the public by a Creative Commons license. The ESV may not be translated in whole or in part into any other language.

Scripture quotations marked CSB have been taken from the Christian Standard Bible®, Copyright © 2017 by Holman Bible Publishers. Used by permission. Christian Standard Bible® and CSB® are federally registered trademarks of Holman Bible Publishers.

Scripture quotations marked HCSB are taken from the Holman Christian Standard Bible®, Copyright © 1999, 2000, 2002, 2003, 2009 by Holman Bible Publishers. Used by permission. Holman Christian Standard Bible®, Holman CSB®, and HCSB® are federally registered trademarks of Holman Bible Publishers.

Scripture quotations marked KJV are from The Authorized (King James) Version. Rights in the Authorized Version in the United Kingdom are vested in the Crown. Reproduced by permission of the Crown's patentee, Cambridge University Press

Scripture quotations marked (NIV) are taken from the Holy Bible, New International Version®, NIV®. Copyright © 1973, 1978, 1984, 2011 by Biblica, Inc.™ Used by permission of Zondervan. All rights reserved worldwide. www.zondervan.com The "NIV" and "New International Version" are trademarks registered in the United States Patent and Trademark Office by Biblica, Inc.™

Scripture verses marked NKJV are taken from the New King James Version®. Copyright © 1982 by Thomas Nelson. Used by permission. All rights reserved.

Scripture quotations marked (NLT) are taken from the Holy Bible, New Living Translation, copyright ©1996, 2004, 2015 by Tyndale House Foundation. Used by permission of Tyndale House Publishers, Carol Stream, Illinois 60188. All rights reserved.

Cover design by twolineSTUDIO.com

ISBN: 978-1-56309-792-8 (paperback)
ISBN: 978-1-56309-793-5 (ebook)

1 2 3 4 5—29 28 27 26 25

"*Fierce* offers young female athletes a powerful blueprint for facing challenges with faith. This devotional demonstrates that God works through our limitations when we put in the work. As a mom of competitive volleyball players, I'm grateful for this resource, which will equip our daughters to compete with the physical strength and spiritual foundation they need both on and off the court." —**Rachel Wojo**, speaker; author of *Desperate Prayers;* volleyball mom

"*Fierce* is a highly inspirational book. It is full of biblical encouragement and empowering stories to equip female athletes to shine brightly and live fearlessly in their sports and beyond." —**Karé Adenegan**, Paralympic silver and bronze medalist

"*Fierce* isn't just a devotional; it's a powerful equipment bag for young female athletes. Packed with practical wisdom and inspiring stories, it fuels faith and empowers them to conquer challenges on and off the field. It is a true game-changer for any young woman in sports." —**Billie Jauss**, author of *Baseball Family*, *Distraction Detox*, and *Making Room*; international speaker; host of *The Family Room* podcast; wife of MLB coach Dave Jauss

"As a mom of a female athlete, I highly recommend *Fierce: Female Athletes Fueled by Faith*. Del Duduit and Caris Snider beautifully blend inspiring stories of female athletes with biblical wisdom, encouraging young women to persevere, honor God, and use their talents for a greater purpose. Each devotional offers powerful lessons on faith, resilience, and character that will inspire my daughter to grow in her sport and spiritual journey. This book is a must-read for any female athlete looking to strengthen her faith and her game. Many blessings to you with this book! It's wonderful!" —**Lori Keating**, award-winning author of *Butterfly Ink*

"*Fierce* is a power-packed dose of inspiration with 52 stories of courageous, faith-filled women who trusted God through the challenges they faced in their respective sports. This book is the practical and spiritual encouragement you need if you're ready to be mentored by incredible female athletes who've turned their fear to faith and their setbacks to comebacks!" —**Michelle Watson Canfield**, PhD, LPC, author of *Let's Talk*; podcast host of *The Dad Whisperer*

"*Fierce* is a powerful reminder that every young female athlete was created on purpose, for a purpose. Through real stories and relatable encouragement, this book helps them see that their identity is not just in what they do on the field but in who they are in Christ. I'm all about resources that point young athletes to their purpose and their Creator. This one does just that!" —**Christen Clark**, host of *The Collide Kids* podcast

"*Fierce: Female Athletes Fueled by Faith* wowed me from the first page. I've long been a fan of female sports, marveling at an ice skater's finesse while performing difficult choreography or cheering a gymnast as she completes the perfect landing. It is evident that female athletes pour their very souls into reaching the top of their chosen sport. That's why I'm so excited about this book! I'm confident it will be a go-to inspirational resource for girls and young women who aspire to become champions in and out of the sports arena.

Fierce features personal accounts of female warriors offering words of wisdom plus a formula for overcoming struggles through perseverance and faith. Reading each chapter is like sitting down with the athlete for a one-on-one discussion. Thank you, Caris and Del, for sharing these competitors' amazing stories through your championship-level storytelling." —**Connie Clyburn**, author of *Wisdom from the Doublewide*

"I highly recommend this book—*Fierce*—for women who want to be fierce and remain godly. We are in a spiritual battle, and we need to be fierce at all times. This devotional gives tools for women to stand firm. I highly recommend this book." —**Cherrilynn Bisbano**, award-winning author

"*Fierce* is filled with both practical application and inspirational stories of faith from some of the best athletes in the world. Their example of how to be fierce, even in adversity, is a great lesson for all of us but especially for female athletes." —**Cade Smith**, Director of Athletics for the University of Alabama in Huntsville

"*Fierce: Female Athletes Fueled by Faith* by Caris Snider and Del Duduit is a book that I can really relate to! As a former college athlete and current avid fan of women's athletics, I enjoyed reading about some of my favorite players. The roster for this great book includes some of my favorite strong females who give their all to their craft while maintaining their faith. I currently coach high school females, and this book is one I will definitely recommend they read!" —**Melissa Knapp**, head coach, girls basketball, Franklin Furnace Green High School

This book is dedicated to young female athletes facing difficulties but continuing to show up every day in a sport God has gifted them with a skill to play. Stay fierce in your faith. Keep competing, thriving, and shining through it all!

CONTENTS

Day 1: YOU 1
Yes, You

Day 2: When God Does What You Can't 5
Paige Bueckers

Day 3: When God Is All You Have 9
Tamika Catchings

Day 4: Free from Fear 15
Sydney McLaughlin-Levrone

Day 5: Never Too Old 21
Laura Wilkinson

Day 6: Embrace Being the Underdog 25
Hezly Rivera

Day 7: What Is God Calling You to Do? 31
Aubrey Kingsbury

Day 8: Let Your Light Shine 37
Rayssa Leal

Day 9: Find Your Joy 41
Jayda Coleman

Day 10: God Is Always Good 45
Mallory Pugh Swanson

Day 11: Stand Firm 49
Lolo Jones

Day 12: God, Guide Me 53
A'ja Wilson

Day 13: Not So Fast 59
Sanya Richards-Ross

Day 14: Why Not You? 65
Jessica Long

Day 15: Your Wake-Up Call 71
Riley Gaines

Day 16: Together in Trials 77
Jill Bohnet

Day 17: You Are More Than 81
Kaley Mudge

Day 18: God's Pleasure 85
Nicola Olyslagers

Day 19: You Just Have to Want It 89
Chantelle Anderson

Day 20: When Struggles Are Best 95
Sabrina Ionescu

Day 21: You Don't Have to Imagine 101
Tobin Heath

Day 22: Get Up 105
Yemisi Ogunleye

Day 23: There Is a Beautiful Peace with God 109
Tamika Catchings

CONTENTS

Day 24: Hiding in the Spotlight 113
Kelsey Plum

Day 25: Are Your Eyes Open? 119
Tori Dilfer

Day 26: Eyes Up 123
Alyssa Brito

Day 27: The Best Day EVER! 129
Hailey Van Lith

Day 28: Fight for Christ 135
Hannah Hidalgo

Day 29: Be Noticed 141
Diana Ordóñez

Day 30: Athlete to Advocate 147
Allyson Felix

Day 31: God Notices You When Others May Not 153
Michelle Moultrie

Day 32: God Loves a Comeback Story 159
Simone Manuel

Day 33: It's Just Better 165
Julie Ertz

Day 34: Drive On 171
Ally McDonald Ewing

Day 35: That's Why It Happened 177
Anna Hall

Day 36: No One Is a Lost Cause 183
Maya Moore

Day 37: Make It a Priority 189
Riley Gaines

Day 38: From the Van Floor to Olympic Stadium 193
Gabby Douglas

Day 39: He Will Get You Through 199
Sanya Richards-Ross

Day 40: Inspire a Generation 205
Karé Adenegan

Day 41: Just Forgive 211
Lolo Jones

Day 42: Building a Sisterhood 217
Felisha Legette-Jack

Day 43: Take Action 223
Grace Lyons Turk

Day 44: Strength in Weakness 227
Kiara Reinhardt

Day 45: You Are Loved, Regardless 233
Jayda Coleman

Day 46: Standing Up by Sitting Out 237
Jaelene Daniels

Day 47: God Will Honor Your Stance 243
Sage Steele

Day 48: Adopted into Hope 249
    Stevey Joy Chapman

Day 49: God Is Confidence 255
    Zoe Snider

Day 50: Time for a Change 259
    Merritt Beason

Day 51: It's Right in Front of You 265
    Allye Snider

Day 52: To Know Christ and Make Him Known 269
    Izzy Nix

Day 1

YOU

Yes, You

By Caris Snider

In the day when I cried out, You answered me,
And made me bold with strength in my soul.
—Psalm 138:3 NKJV

You will read story after story of triumph over tragedy, victory after defeat, and sacrificial stands taken in spite of backlash. Perhaps, you have faced your own circumstances that have brought you to flipping frantically through these pages of black and white searching for guidance on how to be FIERCE in your faith.

These fierce, female athletes do not have a secret sauce consumed in their daily regimen. You will discover not one has lived a trouble-free life. Circumstances will not be conquered using their own capabilities.

Faith fuels their fervent strides forward. God is their source of strength. You will come across Him as the Coach who equipped them to run the race. Their Good Father cheers them on louder than any earthly parent.

He is eager to do the same for you.

Does that mean He is going to put an Olympic gold medal around your neck or a world record in your achievement column? Absolutely not. These accolades may very well fill your shelves one day, but every account absorbed within these pages reveals the driving force for each athlete: Jesus.

They desire to honor Him in every shot taken or finish line crossed. Our fierce females long to point to Jesus for every fan watching and naysayer yelling. These athletes pursue giving God the glory in the face of defeat and the glorious triumphs. Shining His light of hope in the midst of darkness is their objective on every mission field they encounter.

Our mission in passing on every inspirational story is for you to experience God's presence, peace, and power. Each day will leave you with this essential truth: it's your turn to be FIERCE.

> *And when they had prayed, the place in which*
> *they were gathered together was shaken, and they*
> *were all filled with the Holy Spirit and continued*
> *to speak the word of God with boldness.*
>
> —Acts 4:31

Put in the Work

You are ready to be FIERCE. God is not looking for the most educated or talented. He only needs your willingness to step out in faith. God will work through your submission to His plan. How will you take steps forward? What obstacles do you need to face?

Get on the Field

Multiple strategies will be presented to fuel your faith. Numerous struggles will be overcome through similar steps. Day-to-day practical application weaves throughout every story. Here are five reminders to empower your faith.

1. Bible Reading. God's Word is overflowing with actions to incorporate in your life and peaceful words when the trials come. Identify a plan you can do daily. Specify which part of the day, time length, and where you will go to spend important moments with Jesus. "I am the vine; you are the branches. Whoever abides in me and I in him, he it is that bears much fruit, for apart from me you can do nothing" (John 15:5).

2. Prayer. Prayer is our lifeline to the Lord. Kneeling at the altar is not required. Eyes closed and fancy words are not necessary. Crying out to God while driving to work is the right time to pray. Seeking His will for your life first thing in the morning over the opinions of social media is the right time to pray. Talking to Jesus when negative thoughts consume your late-night studies is the right time to pray. You can write your prayers down or say them silently in your soul. Prayer is always right. "Pray without ceasing" (1 Thessalonians 5:17).

3. Arm Bearers. Almost every female athlete you read about has someone in their life whom they can go to in the midst of their toughest challenges. You are not sup-

posed to do life alone. God is not asking you to figure it all out and not use four impactful letters: H E L P. Write down two to three people you can go to who will help carry the heavy load. "Bear one another's burdens, and so fulfill the law of Christ" (Galatians 6:2).

4. Gratitude. God knew the anxieties would be great at times. He made sure to equip us with a simple practice to shift our brains out of this worrisome process. Look for the good around you. Avoid generic groupings and be as specific as possible. Start in the morning while drinking your coffee, and finish your day with thankfulness. Have random moments of gratitude expressed at the dinner table and with your teammates. "Give thanks in all circumstances; for this is the will of God in Christ Jesus for you" (1 Thessalonians 5:18).

5. Help Others. Your skills and talents are not meant just for you. God has gifted you with your ability to reach others. You will encounter someone on the soccer field or behind a desk in desperate need of His love. You will have a teammate in a difficult family situation who will need to know our good Father. You may discover a nonprofit that allows you to do something you love while helping others who feel voiceless. Look for those hidden actions you can take to serve someone knowing it will never be recognized. Go be the hands and feet of Jesus. "For even the Son of Man came not to be served but to serve, and to give his life as a ransom for many" (Mark 10:45).

The time has come to implement the action steps presented on a regular basis. Fuel your faith and unearth a new level of fierce!

Day 2

WHEN GOD DOES WHAT YOU CAN'T

Paige Bueckers

By Caris Snider

But he said, "What is impossible with man is possible with God."

—Luke 18:27

Not too long before Paige Bueckers found herself standing on the basketball court in Portland, Oregon, defeating the women of the University of Southern California (USC) to make it to the Final Four of the 2024 NCAA Women's National Championship, she found herself on a surgeon's table.

A pickup game halted everything for Paige in August of 2022. The news of a torn ACL in her left knee ended her junior season before it ever began. The University of Connecticut (UConn) had just come off of a National Championship run to come up short against the University of South Carolina. Paige had a major setback in front of her, knowing the road to recovery and her ability to get back to her top basketball physique would be almost impossible within her own strength.

This talented home-grown Minnesota basketball player was no stranger to facing a situation that appeared to the outside world as hopeless. In her 2021 season, she experienced a different type of injury in her knee that kept her out of the majority of the season. Paige had to fight her way back from this stumbling block that hindered her from playing the game she loved.

Paige knew the obstacle of this new injury would not be wasted. She took to her Instagram account in August of 2022, saying, "There is going to be good days and there is going to be bad days but my absolute love for the game and Godly strength will get me back to where I need to be."

No one expected Paige and her UConn team to advance past the Sweet Sixteen, much less arrive to the Final Four. She exceeded expectations in spite of the difficulties facing her. In her postgame interview, Paige had this to say, "There's just so much gratitude. I'm a living testimony. I give all glory to God. He works in mysterious ways. Last year I was praying to be back at this stage. He sent me trials and tribulations to build my character and test my faith. I just kept on believing. I did all I could, and God did all I can't."

> *Now to him who is able to do far more*
> *abundantly than all that we ask or think,*
> *according to the power at work within us.*
>
> —Ephesians 3:20

Put in the Work

Paige trusted that God would strengthen her and meet her needs in her process of healing and recovery. She did not allow the pain, setbacks, or doubt-filled thoughts to hold her back from an impossible recovery. Do you find yourself facing an impossible situation? Are you in a circumstance that feels too hard? Is a megaphone shouting in your ear to "Just Give Up"?

Get on the Court

It is not wrong to acknowledge a difficult situation in front of you. God can handle your questions and concerns as you navigate the adversity and unknown. In fact, God wants you to ask for His help and anything else that comes to mind! Having faith in an impossible situation feels scary, but your heavenly Father will help you overcome. Here are some things you can do to walk through the hardship having faith God will do what you can't.

1. Ask Him. Ask God to help you get over this hurdle in your path and to show you how He is using it for good. Grab a pen and journal to write down the answer He reveals. "And we know that for those who love God all things work together for good, for those who are called according to his purpose" (Romans 8:28).

2. Discover the work you can do. We can trust God will do His part, but you have a part to do too! Get honest with yourself and identify three things you need to do as you move forward. If it is an injury, for example, it may be doing the exercises your physical therapist asks

of you. Write down these tasks and remember to do this work as unto the Lord.

3. Express gratitude. Looking for the good even in a bad situation will block your brain from going to a place of worry, anxiety, or defeat. Identify five specific things every day that you are thankful for. Challenge yourself to look for different things, places, or people.

4. Don't give up. When your flesh wants you to walk away, don't give up! When your thoughts tell you it's too hard, don't give up! When others around you say God can't do the impossible anymore, don't give up! Remind yourself that the work He began, He will finish! (Philippians 1:6).

5. Tell your story. We overcome trials and hardships by the blood of the Lamb and the words of our testimony (Revelation 12:11). God is writing a story through you that will help someone else. Write down all that the Lord is doing and be ready to encourage whomever He brings into your path.

You don't have to face adversity alone. God is the same yesterday, today, and forever. He still does the impossible, not just for Paige, but for you!

Day 3
WHEN GOD IS ALL YOU HAVE

Tamika Catchings

By Del Duduit

> *I entreated Your favor with my whole heart;*
> *Be merciful to me according to Your word.*
> *I thought about my ways*
> *and turned my feet to Your testimonies.*
> —Psalm 119:58–59 NKJV

Sometimes God allows you to go through gigantic challenges. Although setbacks are never welcomed, they can be meant for you to rely on the Lord for strength. Sometimes, He wants to be the one you turn to in times of crisis.

Tamika Catchings learned that lesson. The retired WNBA superstar who played for the Indiana Fever grew up in the church and lived a life of faith. But the future WNBA champion and league MVP suffered a season-ending and possible career-ending injury just months before the WNBA draft.

With her future uncertain, there was *one* stable force she leaned on for comfort and encouragement.

The Lord.

Her team, trainers, and fans supported Tamika, but Christ provided the spiritual strength she longed for to recover. She found God was there and gave her peace, joy, and the determination to make it through the setback.

Although she did not play her first year with the Fever, she gained the experience she desired to grow as a Christian. Her faith became stronger, and she realized that the Lord was all she needed in life. During rehabilitation, her priorities shifted to give God glory.

"I think that what I do with my platform is that I live my life as Christlike as I can," Tamika said in an interview with the *Indianapolis Recorder*. "[Jesus] is definitely my savior. He's the one that walks beside me through my ups and downs and the one that keeps me focused on where I am going in life. He protects me. He provides for me. He guides me, and he leads me."

Jesus noticed that and honored her dedication and rewarded her with a glorious career. In 2011, Tamika was voted by fans as one of the Top 15 players in the history of the league. She was a six-time All-Star and helped guide her team to a WNBA championship in 2012.

She was named Finals MVP in 2012 and won five WNBA Defensive Player of the Year awards over her career.

"It seems like every single time I have been hurt, it has been the same thing," she said in an interview with the *Indianapolis Recorder* in 2013. "It's been that you get so caught up in what you are doing that you forget to give Him the glory. It is hard to be a Christian in the WNBA; and I think it is because of so many different stereotypes," she added. "Just trying to walk with Him and not be pulled by all the negative forces from the outside."

Who will you turn to when life gives you a hard foul?

> *The cords of the wicked have bound me,*
> *But I have not forgotten Your law.*
> —Psalm 119:61 NKJV

Put in the Work

You may have your life planned out and as detailed as a scouting report. You might think you are invincible and have your game plan for your life in order. But the devil does not want you to make the clean layup and score. He will cut your legs out from under you while you are in the air. He does not play fair. You may be sure you will be accepted to the college of your dreams, but when you open the email from the university, you are told you won't be attending as you hoped. That special relationship may come to an abrupt end, or you might discover a "friend" is not who you thought they were, and you feel betrayed. Life happens. Setbacks happen.

Get on the Court

How you respond to adversity matters. It's OK to be disappointed and upset when unexpected events happen, but make sure that feeling doesn't go on for days. When you are faced with a life-changing event, what will you do? Will you become angry and question God? Or will you praise Him and accept His path for you? Tamika discovered that if she put her trust in God, He would provide if she honored Him. Here are some ways you can look to Christ in your time of challenge.

1. Cry out. Pour out your tears and frustrations to the Lord. He already knows your feelings and your thoughts—go ahead and let Him hear you. Release your hurt and pain and get it off your chest. Prayer will bring you closer to Him. "In my distress I called upon the Lord / And cried out to my God; / He heard my voice from His temple, / And my cry entered His ears" (2 Samuel 22:7 NKJV).

2. Surrender. The storms you face are too strong for you to handle. Your ego may say you are tough, but the reality is you are human. When you turn it all over to the Lord and seek His help, you will become strong.

3. Work out. Continue to stay healthy. And not in just the physical sense. Do the things you need to do to remain strong in your faith. Continue to read the Word of God and have devotional time. Pray often and attend a solid church on a regular basis. Fellowship is vital.

4. Stay focused. Do not get distracted from your goal. Satan will try to put the full-court press on you and make you turn the ball over. No matter what you want to accomplish, stick to your game plan. "'Therefore wait for Me,' says the Lord, / 'Until the day I rise up for plunder; / My determination is to gather the nations / To My assembly of kingdoms, / To pour on them My indignation / All My fierce anger'" (Zephaniah 3:8 NKJV).

5. Anticipate the return. Just as a doctor will have a discharge plan for you, so does the Savior. You will make it through the storm, and a brighter day will shine. Trust Him.

Tamika's injury did not keep her from a career in the WNBA. It set her back several months, but during that time God prepared her for a wonderful time in professional basketball. Perhaps her injury was a blessing in disguise.

Day 4

FREE FROM FEAR

Sydney McLaughlin-Levrone

By Caris Snider

> *The fear of man lays a snare,*
> *but whoever trusts in the LORD is safe.*
> —Proverbs 29:25

Fast.
Fearless.
Unstoppable.

These are words that come to mind when I think of Sydney McLaughlin-Levrone. Fear of failure is not a term many would use to describe her, but she was held captive by this label for most of her childhood and young adult years.

She recounts in an article she wrote for *Guideposts* a conversation she had with her father at the age of seven. On the way to a race, she told her dad she was terrified of losing. He replied, "If that happens, we'll get some food and go home." His words did not take root in her heart at the time. The more she raced, the more she feared losing. The more she won, the more pressure she felt from the what-ifs of not winning the next one.

The anxiety and terror took its strongest hold during the semi-finals at the 2016 Olympics in Rio during the 400-meter hurdles. There were two other American runners in this race, giving them an opportunity to sweep the competition and take all three spots on the podium. The weight of it all was too much. Sydney found herself pulling back instead of surging during the final seconds to lose and not advance.

For so long, fear had told her if she could not be perfect, there was no sense in trying.

Faith changed everything. She surrendered everything to the Lord from racing to relationships to her fears and anxieties. Her identity was no longer in what she accomplished but in who He said she was. God used wise counsel in her life to help bring about this transformation.

Sydney's coach, Bobby Kersee, gave her a piece of paper with a wheel of emotions. She began to learn how to express what she was feeling even when it was difficult. Andre Levrone Jr., who is now her husband, helped her thrive in her career and faith.

Sydney McLaughlin-Levrone found herself back in the mix during the 2024 Paris Olympics. She finished with two gold medals in the 400-meter hurdles and 4x400-meter relay. She not only walked away with multiple victories but also set a sixth world record in the 400-meter hurdles, running the final race in 50.37 seconds. After winning, she said this, "I credit all that I do to God."

> *Have I not commanded you? Be strong and courageous. Do not be frightened, and do not be dismayed, for the LORD your God is with you wherever you go.*
>
> —Joshua 1:9

Put in the Work

Sydney discovered that freedom from fear was possible. She acknowledged that there was work to do and shifts to make in her thought patterns. This new way of living and thinking was worth it. Do you find yourself trapped in fear? Is the paralysis of perfection holding you back? Are you self-sabotaging out of the thought of failing so you avoid trying at all?

Wear the Medal

It is time to set yourself free from finding your worth and/or identity in a win-loss column. No matter the circumstances that have entangled you in the grips of fear, from a work project to a sport to the thought of comparing yourself to a friend, God has already defined you. He created good works in advance for you to do and no one else. Here are five things you can put into place to overcome fear:

1. Just get the experience. Instead of focusing on results, look to find opportunities. By changing your end goal, this will shift you out of living in a result-oriented mindset. Ask God to help you grow in these situations in your walk with Him and in the gifts and talents you are putting to practice. "Be very careful, then, how you

live—not as unwise but as wise, making the most of every opportunity, because the days are evil" (Ephesians 5:15–16 NIV).

2. Enjoy the work. God wants us to find pleasure in using the skills He has given us. Find ways to have fun and fall in love with what you are doing. Play basketball for the joy of the game. Go to school with the excitement of learning something new. Drive to your job knowing God has given you a gift and you have the privilege of putting it to use. "For even the Son of Man came not to be served but to serve, and to give his life as a ransom for many" (Mark 10:45).

3. Identify your emotions. God gave us the gift to feel different emotions. It isn't that our emotions are bad. The problem comes when we push them down and don't acknowledge they are there. Throughout today, practice saying out loud what you are feeling. It could be uncomfortable at first, but once you start, it will help you get out of the fog and into clarity. Take a breath and ask God to help you handle your emotions in a healthier way.

4. Stay with it. This process will take time. Making changes to step out of fear and into freedom will be much like throwing spaghetti. You will find what sticks and you will run the race of life as a marathon now instead of a sprint.

5. Think on what *is*. The what-ifs of fear can cause us to spiral if we follow them down the rabbit hole. When the what-ifs start to play out, PAUSE. Use a notebook

DAY 4: FREE FROM FEAR

or the notes section in your phone and write out these thoughts. Take the next step that Philippians 4:8 tells us and think on what *is* true, honorable, just, pure, lovely, commendable, excellent, and worthy of praise.

You don't have to be controlled by fear any longer. God has cut you loose from the bondage of dread working overtime to steal from your life. It is time to walk in freedom!

Day 5

NEVER TOO OLD

Laura Wilkinson

By Caris Snider

And it shall come to pass afterward, / that I will pour out my Spirit on all flesh; / your sons and your daughters shall prophesy, / your old men shall dream dreams, / and your young men shall see visions.

—Joel 2:28

Waste of space. That is what Laura Wilkinson was called when she was kicked off her school's diving team in high school. She took her first dive off a ten-meter platform at fifteen and was told she was too old to begin in diving. One year later, she won her first national title, earned a spot on the US National Team, and stood on the platform with a bronze medal at the World Cup.

Laura refused to allow the timeline from others to determine what she could accomplish. Her career has been filled with moments of beating the odds.

Wilkinson was doing her normal warm-up for the 2000 Olympic trials when an obstacle emerged. She suffered an injury, breaking her right foot in three places. The only way to fix it and allow the foot to heal properly was through a rebreak conducted by the doctor. She overcame the setback to make it to the Olympics, but battling through the pain proved to be difficult.

Laura found herself in eighth place after the semifinals. Down sixty points, she recorded one of the biggest upsets in Olympic history. She persevered and won the gold at her first Olympic appearance with two and a half somersaults and a half twist.

This mom of four came out of nine years of retirement for the 2020 Olympics, longing to get back on the platform. Training revealed a dangerous issue going on in her neck. Hitting the water at high rates of speed had caused damage to her spinal cord. After surgery, she went straight back to training.

Wilkinson has never been distracted by injury, opinions, or age. At forty-three, she walked onto the ten-meter platform with her four children cheering her on at the 2021 Olympic Trials.

Laura shares, "When I became a mom, I don't know if it's a culture thing or it's just something as a mom you get into your head that, 'my time is over and now it's time to just be there for my kids,' it's so not true. You can have kids and you can have big dreams and do things and bring them along for the ride. When they get to watch you and be part of that experience with you, I mean, that speaks so much louder to them than if you just tell them how to live. If they can actually see you doing it, that makes a bigger, lasting impression."

> *O God, from my youth you have taught me, / and I still proclaim your wondrous deeds. / So even to*

*old age and gray hairs, / O God, do not forsake
me, / until I proclaim your might to another
generation, / your power to all those to come.*
—Psalm 71:17–18

Put in the Work

The old adage "age is just a number" rang true for Laura Wilkinson. Not once did a number factor into her decision to face fear and leap in the air toward her dream. What dreams have you put on the shelf due to the idea of being the wrong age? What is truly holding you back if you were to be honest with yourself?

Get on the Platform

Laura tuned out the naysayers. She endured the pain by keeping the end game in sight. She saw every opportunity as a way for others to experience God's love and power. Here are some steps you can take to dust off those shelf dreams.

1. Remove your age. God gives us example after example in His Word of using people in all age groups. If the Lord doesn't classify how to use us through this lens, you can remove this restriction. It has never been about an era for Him. The stirring in your spirit is not an accident. The time is now. "For I can do everything through Christ, who gives me strength" (Philippians 4:13 NLT).
2. Remove your doubt. What doubts are bombarding your mind? Take sixty seconds to write down every single doubt bombarding your thoughts. Next, search the Scriptures to find truth to combat these uncertainties.
3. Remove your fears. Fear is a popular topic when it comes to searching for scripture. How to combat it and

remove it from one's life affects more than you and me. Fear has held you back long enough. It no longer gets to use false evidence or lies to trap you. Sometimes the best way to remove fear is to face it. "Fear not, for I am with you; / be not dismayed, for I am your God; / I will strengthen you, I will help you, / I will uphold you with my righteous right hand" (Isaiah 41:10).

4. Remove opinions. Get ready for everyone's opinion when you take the plunge! Friends you have not spoken to in years will have all the reasons for why this will never work. Social media keyboard warriors will slide into your messages with the most negative words they can find. Permission to not give their opinions a response! Move on in action. You will never know what will happen unless you try.

5. Remove results. It is not about the results. Taking this leap of faith is more about your response to living life instead of staying on the sidelines of safety. God-sized dreams will require you to lean on Him for the results. They will also cause you to take steps out of your comfort zone. God is asking you to trust in His strength. "But they who wait for the LORD shall renew their strength; / they shall mount up with wings like eagles; / they shall run and not be weary; / they shall walk and not faint" (Isaiah 40:31).

It's never too late to chase a dream! You never know who is standing behind you watching you and cheering you on. Your biggest supporters could be the tiniest voices with the greatest belief. Seize this moment to leave an impression on them.

Day 6

EMBRACE BEING THE UNDERDOG

Hezly Rivera

By Caris Snider

*Don't let anyone look down on you because you
are young, but set an example for the believers in
speech, in conduct, in love, in faith and in purity.*
—1 Timothy 4:12 NIV

When Hezly Rivera hit her sweet sixteen, she embraced the intimidation of big lights, uneven bars, and a four-inch beam to make the 2024 US Olympic Gymnastics Team. Age or fear were not going to derail her from achieving her goal. Even though she was labeled an underdog and a long shot, Hezly was steadfast through the pressure. She became the youngest athlete competing for Team USA at the Paris Olympics.

This New Jersey native discovered her passion for the sport at a gymnastics-themed birthday party. Between eating cake and cartwheeling on the floor, coaches noticed a talent in this five-year-old little girl. Her family supported the dream Hezly was working toward and moved to Plano, Texas, to begin training at the World Olympic Gymnastics Academy in 2022.

The small number of years Hezly Rivera has had on this earth has never held her back. She does not minimize what she can do from the words of older experts around her. In an interview with Rose Minutaglio from *ELLE*, she says, "I'm capable and can do anything I put my mind to." Focusing on what she can control and not on the trials in front of her keeps her confidence steady to continue forward.

Even when multiple gymnasts faced injuries during the Olympic Trials, Hezly put her hope and trust in God into action. Her faith provides a key element to keep her mind clear and engaged for every new milestone achieved. Prayer with her family and Christian music uplifts her spirit as she prepares for each meet. She does not shy away from vocalizing how God helps her show up on the mat every day to better her skills.

She took to Instagram after her team secured the gold medal, sharing a picture of the girls embracing with a simple message: "Olympic gold medalist. Couldn't be more thankful and super proud of this team."

> *But those who hope in the LORD*
> *will renew their strength.*
> *They will soar on wings like eagles;*
> *they will run and not grow weary,*
> *they will walk and not be faint.*
> —Isaiah 40:31 NIV

Put in the Work

Hezly had no doubt God had prepared her to go and do what some thought she was too young and ill-prepared to handle. She kept her focus on the moment in front of her and what she could control instead of the noise surrounding her. Do you find that you are holding back from using your gifts and talents because someone has told you that you are too young? Are you feeling caught in the middle of fear and faith? Do you find yourself longing to be used by God right now but you don't know how to speak up?

Wear the Medal

God is not in the business of putting age restrictions on when and how He can use you. He shows us throughout scripture that it doesn't matter what era you are in. Our heavenly Father is looking for those willing and ready to go to work. The good news is that He knows what is in you, from every ability to every weakness. He's not asking you to be the best, oldest, or strongest. He is holding your hand as you embrace being an underdog. Here are some steps you can take as you move forward in setting an example in living the life God has for you:

1. Acknowledge what you are feeling. Talk to God about the fear or anxieties you may be feeling. Let Him know where you are feeling weak so His mercy and grace will be strong. Write this down as a prayer in your Bible or prayer journal and date it. Come back to it from time to time to chart your growth as He gives you the courage you need. "But he said to me, 'My grace is sufficient for

you, for my power is made perfect in weakness'" (2 Corinthians 12:9 NIV).

2. Go and do it. Yes, you can. You can do this. God does not make a mistake in what He is asking you to do. If it seems big and scary, that is not a sign it is not meant for you. Instead, it is an opportunity for you to place your trust in Him and go and do something outside of yourself that will impact others. Determine one scary step God is asking you to take. It might be trying a new position in a sport you play or inviting your friend to church. Remember, He is not asking for perfection, just the willingness to try. Write it down and give yourself a deadline.

3. Look for the controllables. When the distractions come and the naysayers are loud, focus your thoughts on what you can control. This will allow you to stay on task and to continue moving forward in peace in the midst of chaos. Use your senses and identify one thing you can see, hear, taste, touch, and smell. Stay present. (Philippians 4:8)

4. Have support. You were not meant to do this life alone. Finding adults you can look to for advice and encouragement will be so helpful in walking out the life God has for you no matter your age. Who are three people you can reach out to when it gets difficult? Reach out to them and ask them if they are willing to walk this journey with you. "Bear one another's burdens, and so fulfill the law of Christ" (Galatians 6:2 NKJV).

5. See your opportunities. God has given you the gifts and talents you have to bring others to Him. Every at bat you face, game-winning goal you kick, or gut-punching defeat you experience, use it to point your peers to Jesus.

You don't have to wait until you're older to make an impact. God is calling you to go in faith and do what some may call a long shot. He will give you the courage you need. Your time is right now!

Day 7

WHAT IS GOD CALLING YOU TO DO?

Aubrey Kingsbury

By Del Duduit

My sheep hear my voice, and I know them, and they follow me.

—John 10:27

Life is a blur for most people. Not just amature or professional athletes like Aubrey Kingsbury. Everyone's schedule can be hectic. If you are a college student, then you face deadlines and testing that can apply pressure on you. And if you are in today's fast-paced job market, you are well aware of the demands that everyone faces.

Aubrey was no exception. She faced demands on her time and energy. She was one of three goalies selected to the US Soccer Team. The two-time National Women's Soccer League Goalkeeper of the Year with the Washington Spirit and the 2021 NWSL Champ received her first national team notification in

2019. Aubrey made her only appearance against Uzbekistan in 2022 and was able to be part of the team that qualified for the World Cup.

The Cincinnati, Ohio, native grew up in a Christian home and knew the benefits of living a life of faith. Although playing on a national stage has implications of stardom, the Wake Forest University alum knows she is not defined by what happens on the field of play.

"The Lord is calling us to a life of freedom and joy, and I was missing out on that by thinking I already had it through what the world tells you matters," Aubrey told *Sports Spectrum* in 2019. "Once I learned that it's not about my performance and I could rest in Christ's performance on the cross, it just opened my eyes."

Those are easy words to say and difficult to live out at times. But Aubrey has proved them to be true. She has maintained a focus on prayer that has proven to be a source of strength.

"I would say my prayer kind of this whole year has just been, 'Lord, help me cast my desires and wishes aside and just take up what You have for me,'" she said. "Just kind of a daily humbling of myself and submitting to His plan and trying to see my teammates through His eyes and love and serve those around me regardless of what role I have."

What does God have for you? How can you know for sure what He has in store?

> *When the Spirit of truth comes, he will guide you into all the truth, for he will not speak on his own authority, but whatever he hears he will speak, and he will declare to you the things that are to come.*
>
> —John 16:13

Put in the Work

Maybe you are wondering what God has in store for you and the future. You might be concerned or frustrated because others around you appear to have their life in order. Perhaps you are undecided about what college to attend or what job to take or what relationship to enter. Maybe you trust God and are a Christian but don't have the direction you long for from the Master. Does it anger you when someone tells you to "just be patient. It will happen"?

Get on the Pitch

Life is a challenge. Your family and friends are making the teams, and you sit on the sideline waiting to get into the game. You have prayed and fasted and put in the time, but your name is not called. How can you know what God has for you when you don't hear anything from Him? Sound familiar? Here are some things to do while you wait on His timing and direction.

1. Resist feelings of anger and frustration. Easier said than done, right? When you pray and wait and wait and pray, feelings of impatience can mount. But know that God *is* working and does have a plan for you. Perhaps He is waiting on you to turn your doubts over to Him. You are heard. Just know that something big is coming. Instead of frustration, turn that emotion into excitement.

2. Experience God's goodness while you wait. When you focus on the problems and not on the solution, your time can be eaten up by the devil. Satan wants to distract you and tell you that God has forgotten about you.

Turn the tables on the enemy and focus on the goodness of God. Your life may have challenges, but it also has positive aspects. Show God gratitude and thank Him instead of complaining. "The Lord is good, / a stronghold in the day of trouble, / he knows those who take refuge in him" (Nahum 1:7).

3. Work out and practice. All Olympians practice their entire lives for one moment where they can be the best. And, for some, that moment may never come. An injury may keep them from participating in an event they have worked years to reach. But they still practice. While you wait, dive into God's Word. Pray to Him more without asking for things and attend His house to worship.

4. Occupy your time. Give back. This shows yourself and the Lord that your needs are not what matters to you. Volunteer at a homeless shelter or deliver food to people in need. Help someone get on their feet or donate your time at a food bank.

5. Anticipate. A good athlete makes great plays when they anticipate what their opponents will do. They watch tapes of previous games and study their opposition. When you are one step ahead of the forces of evil and trust God's game plan, life will work out. Anticipate the Lord's favor on you and rejoice when it's revealed. "But seek first the kingdom of God and his righteousness, and all these things will be added to you" (Matthew 6:33).

Knowing what God has planned for you can be a mystery at times. But when you actively search for His will and are patient, God will reveal Himself and His plans for you. It may not be in your time, but that is an issue for you to work on and gain strength at the same time.

Day 8

LET YOUR LIGHT SHINE

Rayssa Leal

By Caris Snider

Jesus said to him, "I am the way, and the truth, and the life. No one comes to the Father except through me."

—John 14:6

What would you do if you were told you could not acknowledge your faith? What if those in authority over you tried to pressure you into silence? How would you respond?

Rayssa Leal found herself in this situation. The sixteen-year-old skateboarder from Brazil was allegedly told she could not outwardly praise Jesus at the 2024 Paris Olympics.

This was not her first opportunity to be on the world stage showcasing her talent and skills on a skateboard. Famous skateboarder Tony Hawk shared a video of her as a kid skateboarding and doing unbelievable tricks dressed as a blue fairy princess. During the 2021 Olympics, she earned a silver medal for the first ever street skateboarding competition during the games.

Fast-forward to Place de La Concorde, where Rayssa would once again get a moment in time to reveal her artistry on the board. After hearing the announcement that she was on the podium with the bronze medal, Rayssa made a decision. She put her courage muscle into action and used sign language to quote John 14:6, letting the world know Jesus *is* the way!

Her creative thinking to acknowledge *truth* went viral. No matter the bushel the world may have tried to put over the light in Rayssa Leal, Jesus shined brighter.

> *Go therefore and make disciples of all nations, baptizing them in the name of the Father and of the Son and of the Holy Spirit, teaching them to observe all that I have commanded you. And behold, I am with you always, to the end of the age.*
>
> —Matthew 28:19–20

Put in the Work

Rayssa knew God deserved the glory that day in the hot July sun. She had no doubt the skill set she had was from Him, and He opened the door for her to assert His sovereignty. Do you find yourself standing at a juncture where people around you are trying to silence your faith? Are you in a situation where you know God is calling on you to be a witness for Him, but you are scared?

Wear the Medal

You are not alone if standing up for your faith feels intimidating. Many Christians believe they don't have the right words or know enough scripture to stand firm when the time comes. Thankfully, God does not put the requirement of perfection or total memorization of the Bible to go be salt and light in our corners of the world. He will be with us when those chances come to speak up for Him. Here are practical steps to put in place to daily shine bright:

1. Start with a small step. Ask God to help you see the easily missed opportunities to illuminate His love for those around you. He might lead you to pray over your lunch at school, start a Bible study with your sports team, or ask a coworker to go to church with you. Pick one small step, see how it goes, then take another. "Therefore, my dear brothers and sisters, stand firm. Let nothing move you. Always give yourselves fully to the work of the Lord, because you know that your labor in the Lord is not in vain" (1 Corinthians 15:58 NIV).

2. Put on the armor. When our soldiers go into battle, they are prepared. They get their gear on and weapons ready for any possible attack. We know our enemy wants to steal, kill, and destroy. He wants to back us into a corner, and we must be ready. Every day, get in God's Word and put on the armor He has given us. "Put on the full armor of God, so that you can take your stand against the devil's schemes" (Ephesians 6:11 NIV).

3. Resist doubt. Can I be honest? This is the step that trips me up the most. My thoughts cause me to doubt I can take a bold stand for Jesus. I get caught up in getting my words wrong or saying something that doesn't make sense, so I say nothing at all. Thankfully, God is not asking us to be their Savior—He has that covered. He just needs us to push through the doubts, open our mouths, and trust He will put the words and actions in motion. Take the pressure off of getting it right and switch to being obedient.

4. Go in a group. There is power in numbers! Having friends with you on this adventure can help you resist any opposition you will face. Talk to some of your comrades and decide what your game plan will be to share the love of Jesus. "Resist him, standing firm in the faith, because you know that the family of believers throughout the world is undergoing the same kind of sufferings" (1 Peter 5:9 NIV).

5. Write your testimony. God has given you a story to share. It doesn't have to be filled with tumultuous dead ends or tragedy you overcame. It may be that you came to know Christ during vacation Bible school as a child, and you have walked with Him through the difficulties of middle school to high school and now another young girl needs to hear this story. Don't demean what He has done in you. Someone out there is waiting to hear this good news.

Let's put our creativity to use like Rayssa. The world needs blazing flames.

Day 9

FIND YOUR JOY

Jayda Coleman

By Del Duduit

These things I have spoken to you, that My joy may remain in you, and that your joy may be full.

—John 15:11 NKJV

You would think that helping your team to win a College World Series Championship in softball is a big deal. And it is. With it comes prestige and accomplishment and honor. But those feelings fade, and the awards gather dust at some point and people forget.

That's why Jayda Coleman, a superb softball player, finds her reward in her faith in Jesus Christ. When she helped spark her Oklahoma Sooners to four College World Series Championships, she said those titles were great, but did not mean the world to her.

"I was just so happy that we won the College World Series, but I didn't feel joy," she said in an article in *Sports Spectrum* after the first championship. "I didn't know what to do the next day. I didn't know what to do for that following week. I didn't feel filled, and I had to find Christ in that."

She was proud of her accomplishment on the field and for her teammates because they made it to the top of women's college sports. But there is a fine line. For Jayda, her inner peace comes through her relationship with her Savior.

"I had to find something that fulfills me in my heart, regardless of if we win or if we three-peat or if we don't," Jayda said in *The Atlantic*. "I'm still going to be fulfilled in my heart, because reading my Bible at night and praying to God is what fulfills me, not winning a national championship."

Success on the softball field can provide a sense of accomplishment. But it cannot provide peace and fulfillment. Jayda knows where that is found.

> *Now may the God of hope fill you with all joy*
> *and peace in believing, that you may abound in*
> *hope by the power of the Holy Spirit.*
> —Romans 15:13 NKJV

Put in the Work

Where do joy and peace come from in your life? There is nothing wrong with feeling good about a productive day at work. That job promotion might be a signal from your employer that you are doing a great job. Or that sense of pride you get when your kids do something good, and it reflects back on you. Big events in life are to be honored and appreciated. But you cannot rely on those to deliver peace and joy in your life.

Get on the Field

Peace and joy are intangibles. They cannot come from anything this world has to offer. They can bring happiness for a moment, but those moments fade. Being happy is one thing. Having peace and joy is another. What brings you peace in your life? What brings you joy? A budding romance can be satisfying and lead to a happy life. A new job can invite a sense of adventure. But do they provide peace and joy? Not really. Here are some ways you can enjoy life and maintain peace and joy on your journey.

1. A sense of gratitude. In the Word of God, Christ discusses ways to give thanks often for your blessings. Gratitude is a mindset that helps to transform your mental state into one of peace and joy. When you are grateful for what you have earned, then God will bless you with true joy.

2. Make time for quiet. Set aside time each week or even each day to silence distractions around you. Turn off your phone during devotions or take a break from social media after a certain point in the day. This will take away all the bombardments in your life and allow you some free time to concentrate on God's goodness in your life. Even ten minutes a day will do wonders. Find peace in silence. "Let the word of Christ dwell in you richly in all wisdom, teaching and admonishing one another in psalms and hymns and spiritual songs, singing with grace in your hearts to the Lord" (Colossians 3:16 NKJV).

3. Have a solid circle of friends. Friendship and companionship are vital in having peace and joy. True friends

will be there in the ups and downs. They will also tell you when they think you are messing up and applaud you when you do good. Friends can keep you grounded and provide a sense of belonging. Community brings peace.

4. Serve others. When you take time to help someone who is less fortunate than you, it's not pity. When you serve others, whether it be at a clothing bank or homeless shelter or food pantry, you find a sense of joy. Christ has blessed you in many ways. And when you give back, He rewards you with joy. "And whatever you do in word or deed, do all in the name of the Lord Jesus, giving thanks to God the Father through Him" (Colossians 3:17 NKJV).

5. Have fun. Life is too short to be angry. You will experience times of unhappiness and trouble, but when you possess a joyful heart, Christ will provide you with strength and encouragement to face life's challenges. No matter what you do in life, whether it's work or play, have fun. "Beloved, I pray that you may prosper in all things and be in health, just as your soul prospers" (3 John 1:2 NKJV).

Jayda had fun in her college softball career. She won four College World Series Championships and was named First Team All-American three times. That has to be fun. But she also knew that would be for a short season. Her joy and peace through her relationship with Jesus Christ will last a lifetime here on earth and forever in heaven.

Day 10

GOD IS ALWAYS GOOD

Mallory Pugh Swanson

By Caris Snider

Consider it a great joy, my brothers and sisters, whenever you experience various trials, because you know that the testing of your faith produces endurance.

—James 1:2–3 CSB

Turbulent trials brought Mallory Pugh Swanson to a screeching halt in her soccer career. She contemplated early retirement at the age of twenty-three after sustaining multiple injuries. During all the setbacks, she endured with an upturn in her play. Mallory was gearing up for a run at the World Cup in 2023 with the USWNT when a major blow to her resurgence happened.

She tore her left patellar tendon during a match against Ireland on April 8, 2023. After surgery, she found herself in an emergency with infection spreading and needing a second surgery. In the midst of all she lost, she kept her focus on God's goodness. She took to her Instagram page and shared with her fans, "The beauty of all of this is that God is always good. He's got me and always has."

Mallory began one of the greatest comebacks the sport had seen. She found herself on the Olympic team during the Paris 2024 games. During the gold medal match against Brazil, it took fifty-seven minutes for the winning goal to be scored. Mallory was the one who found the seam to make it happen.

She was an important piece of the puzzle in the American women making this historic run. Mallory told NBC's Mike Tirico after the match, "We've been playing with joy, and you can just see it on the field."

Her husband, Major League Baseball player Dansby Swanson, was back at home playing with the Cubs cheering her on. He summed up her comeback by reflecting on God's hand in her journey: "In God's beauty and brilliance, He can take something that's so devastating and create something even more amazing than one could ever imagine!"

> *You intended to harm me, but God intended it*
> *for good to accomplish what is now being done,*
> *the saving of many lives.*
>
> —Genesis 50:20 NIV

Put in the Work

There was a point where Mallory asked God why all the trials and difficulties were happening to her. In the midst of her frustration, God showed up with a simple answer. He helped her to see the good in the hard because it was building up her faith and trust in Him. Like Mallory, have you found yourself in the midst of a hard season asking God, Why? Are you trying to understand what is going on in your life but you wonder if you will ever get on the right path? Are you contemplating walking away from all God has for you because you don't see the end in sight?

Wear the Medal

God can handle your why moment. You don't have to shy away from the messy questions and tears in your heavenly Father's presence. Building up your ability to persevere in this life takes time. Here are some things you can do to move through the setbacks and start your comeback:

1. Get back up. Yes, it might be hard, but if God still has you here, He is not done yet. Perhaps you find yourself recovering from a painful injury. Maybe you have experienced a major setback at work. Whatever the trial, lean on your faith and ask the Holy Spirit to strengthen you to keep going. "That He would grant you, according to the riches of His glory, to be strengthened with might through His Spirit in the inner man" (Ephesians 3:16 NKJV).

2. Look for the good. Finding the good in the midst of tough times is no easy task, but putting in the effort to see things differently will help your brain to think with new pathways. God has given us the authority to take our thoughts captive and to be in charge of where they go. Intentionally look for the good in your situation. It may be something as simple as getting your favorite

candy after a surgery to a more in-depth view of seeing your trust growing in God's plan for your life.

3. Endure the pressure. Pressure is not easy, but it is a privilege. Diamonds need extreme conditions to be formed. God knows the beauty on the other side of the pain. Write in your prayer journal a prayer of belief, trusting God has something incredible waiting on the other side. "But He knows the way that I take; When He has tested me, I shall come forth as gold" (Job 23:10 NKJV).

4. Have a support system. Mallory often shares how her husband held her up and encouraged her during the rocky journey of recovery. You were not meant to bear the burden alone. Reach out to three friends and ask them to walk with you.

5. Find the joy. Multiple teammates of Mallory spoke about the joy she played with during the gold medal match. Joy is there, right now, for you. It is steadfast in chaos and catching to others around you. Joy will bring you to a place of contentment as you surrender and trust God's plan and timing. Night will make way for the morning!

If Mallory Pugh Swanson had walked away when tragedy struck, she would have missed out on the windfall of God's steadfast faithfulness. Do not stop now. You have made it this far! Keep walking forward to see how God will use it for good!

Day 11

STAND FIRM

Lolo Jones

By Del Duduit

Watch, stand fast in the faith, be brave, be strong.
—1 Corinthians 16:13 NKJV

Scripture tells you to be brave and strong and hold to your faith. But could you have gone through what Lolo Jones did and still be brave and strong? The Olympian star has been dragged through the media mud and made fun of all because she chose to be true to her Lord and Savior.

Lolo, a multidecorated athlete from Louisiana State University, is unique because she had trained for and participated in both the Summer and Winter Olympics games.

On August 4, 2012, Lolo was criticized by a writer for the *The New York Times* because of her status as a single female and not for her athletic abilities. Lolo is an attractive lady, and the author of the article suggested that her fame was due to her looks and not her achievements. The article also compared her to tennis star Anna Kournikova, whom the author stated never won a WTA singles tournament but became famous for appearing in numerous photo shoots and magazines and advertisements due to her looks. The author was wrong because Kournikova had won tournaments on the WTA circuit but failed to report that fact.

Instead of having a popular dating life, Lolo said she wanted to stay a virgin until marriage and that was why some media made fun of her and her beliefs.

"I got raked over the coals for my faith," she said during a press conference before she spoke at an event sponsored by the Fellowship of Christian Athletes. "That was hard on me. You can be celebrated if you say you are LGBTQ, but then you are destroyed if you say you don't want to have sex before marriage—completely destroyed. It was frustrating with the double standard. Some nights I cried my eyes out for sure and prayed. I felt attacked and embarrassed."

She still is a target of attacks for standing on her beliefs—what the Bible teaches.

"Still get attacked today for not having sex before marriage," she added. "It is one of the biggest frustrations I've had."

How would you stand up to public attacks?

> *Who are you to judge another's servant? To his own master he stands or falls. Indeed, he will be made to stand, for God is able to make him stand.*
>
> —Romans 14:4 NKJV

Put in the Work

Life is tough enough without being criticized for what you believe in as a Christian. You will face persecution. But how much public criticism could you take? How would you hold up as a hit piece ran on you in one of the world's largest circulated publications? Would you feel like crawling into a hole and hiding? Lolo faced the world stage in the Olympic games after being criticized for waiting to have sex after marriage.

Wear the Medal

Will you give in to public criticism? You may never compete for a gold medal in the Olympics, so let's get down to your level. Perhaps your boss yelled at you in front of your colleagues. Maybe you serve on a public board and have faced criticism for a decision you made or a vote you cast. Perhaps you are a coach and have issues getting that first win, and the parents want you fired. How will your faith hold up? Or maybe you are just like Lolo and want to wait until marriage to have a sexual relationship but are getting pressure from friends. Here are some tips to keep your faith when you are under attack.

1. Find strength in the situation. Remember the common adage "No pain, no gain." You will go through things in life you don't understand. But when you find the situation a source of strength to provide determination to keep going, you have the right attitude. The Lord will allow some circumstances to come into your life to make you stronger. "He gives power to the weak, And to

those who have no might He increases strength" (Isaiah 40:29).

2. Never back down. Never give your enemies water to toss on your fire. Believe it or not, they do not want you to give in to their demands. They look up to you in a bizarre way. How you act under pressure will show them God. You are the best example of the Bible they will see.

3. Find sources of support. Talk to your pastor or coach or friends or parents. There are support groups out there for you. It's OK to vent and talk. But also, don't forget to pray to the Lord.

4. Take a break. Sometimes you just need to get away from the moment. Find a good book like the Bible and delve into what the Word of God says. Take a long weekend or just get away from those who are chasing you. Don't run away from your problems, but it's OK to take a break and recharge.

5. Keep your faith. Find out what the Lord says about your situation. You can find it in scripture. Also find what fuels your faith. If it's Christian music, then build your faith with that. "The Lord is my strength and my shield; / My heart trusted in Him, and I am helped; / Therefore my heart greatly rejoices, / And with my song I will praise Him" (Psalm 28:7 NKJV).

Lolo stuck to her beliefs and, although she was ridiculed, she was also admired. Someone is watching how you react to a negative situation. Be the reason someone is inspired and motivated by your faith.

Day 12

GOD, GUIDE ME

A'ja Wilson

By Caris Snider

But I trust in you, O LORD;
I say, "You are my God."
—Psalm 31:14

Growing up in church became the cement that helped shape A'ja Wilson into the person she is on and off the basketball court. Her grandfather was the minister at Saint John Baptist Church in Columbia, South Carolina, where this formation began. Her parents, aunts, uncles, and friends mentored her in the truth of God's Word for the days when difficulties would come.

A'ja's sophomore year of high school brought an unexpected battle when she was diagnosed with dyslexia, a learning disability that can affect a person's ability to read and write. Determination set in, and she and her parents refused to allow this to be a weakness. In 2019, they created the A'ja Wilson Foundation to help change the stigma of dyslexia for this younger generation.

Her work ethic, which she attributes to her grandmother, Hattie Rakes, kicked in. A'ja's dedication to working through the not-so-glamorous parts of life brought her to the University of South Carolina, where, in her junior season, she contributed a vital role to the first National Championship win in the history of the program. During her time as a Gamecock, she pushed herself to saying grace before meals and reading scripture in front of the team pregame in the locker room. This helped build her confidence as a leader and her diligence in not being held back by a label.

As a member of the Aces WNBA team in Las Vegas, she keeps her mind focused on God ordering her steps. In an interview after one of her games, A'ja reflected on God equipping her with everything she needs for the moment—nothing more, nothing less—and that He is ordering her steps. She concluded the interview by saying, "My prayer every day is, God, guide me."

A'ja Wilson has made history by becoming a three-time MVP, a two-time Olympic gold medalist, and winning back-to-back WNBA championships. Her trust in God's plan and being obedient to wherever He leads, keeps her grounded. She knows that the Lord will give and take away, and through it all, she will trust in His plan.

In an interview with *Sports Spectrum*, A'ja had this to say: "The road's not going to be easy and it's not going to be glamorous. That's what I have to continue to understand—that God is in control."

> *The steps of a man are established by the* L<small>ORD</small>,
>   *when he delights in his way;*

> *though he fall, he shall not be cast headlong,*
> *for the L*ORD *upholds his hand.*
> —Psalm 37:23–24

Put in the Work

Eva Wilson, A'ja's mom, often tells her, "God's plan in God's time." This steady reminder helps A'ja to stay the course and trust God will give her one step at a time as she needs it. Are you standing at a crossroads not knowing which way you are supposed to go? Do you sense God is asking you to take a step forward in obedience but not knowing the next five steps is halting your movement? Have you found that the noise around you is so loud it keeps you from doing the work you are capable of doing?

Wear the Medal

God is faithful to His Word. When He shows you a step to take, you can trust He never makes a mistake. The Lord knows the good plans for your life. When you follow His direction, it may lead down a winding path, but it will be worth it to go where He leads! Here are some practices you can begin to implement to help you do the not-so-glamorous parts while trusting in God to do the impossible parts.

1. Surrender. Without taking this step, none of the others will matter. Surrender control to God. Take a moment on your knees and give everything to Him that you have been trying to hide, fix, or force to happen. His plan and His way are so much better. "'For I know the plans I have for you,' declares the LORD, "plans to pros-

per you and not to harm you, plans to give you hope and a future'" (Jeremiah 29:11 NIV).

2. Take the first step. A'ja shared how asking God to guide her steps helps her every day from the court to interactions with the youth in her community. He will be steadfast in revealing the steps for us to take. It could be putting extra work in during practice to earn a starting position. Perhaps, He is leading you to talk to your neighbor who just lost their spouse and pray for them. The first step He gives you may be to fill out a college application, trusting He will provide the finances. Take the step, not focusing on the results but rather focusing on being obedient to Him.

3. Tune out the noise. Have you found that the negative people around you seem to come out of nowhere when you begin to walk out your faith? The outside noise will never stop. We can tune it out by focusing on the game of life we are playing. Pleasing God rather than man will help with this step. Remind yourself you are seeking His applause. Keep this your focus and He will cheer you on. "So whether we are at home or away, we make it our aim to please him" (2 Corinthians 5:9).

4. Stand firm. Even when the naysayers come at you, do not waiver in the steps you know God has put in your path. To keep your feet unyielding, memorize scripture. You can choose a new verse every week, month, or however best you can learn it. When the negative words come, you can take them captive with the living and active word of God.

5. Help others. A'ja's teammates and coach speak highly of her ability to lead others and take them along with her. When we look for ways to serve those around us, we are following the example of Christ. As He walked out the path His Father had for Him, He was always looking for ways to serve rather than be served. Who is one person you can lend a helping hand to today?

The things God has allowed A'ja Wilson to do did not happen overnight. Practice, focus, and a willingness to do the hard work were all key values in getting to where she is, but trusting He is in control has kept her moving forward. Are you ready to concede your will to God's?

Day 13

NOT SO FAST

Sanya Richards-Ross

By Del Duduit

*Blessed are those who keep his testimonies,
who seek him with their whole heart.*
—Psalm 119:2

Being fast was a way of life for Sanya Richards-Ross. She is one of the fastest American women in history to be exact. Sanya set the record for the fastest 400-meter dash and became the first American woman in almost three decades to be an Olympic champion in the 400 meter while at the Olympics in 2012 in London. She won the crown by dashing past her competitors in the final fifty meters of the race to win in an exciting finish.

She won her fourth gold medal and anchored the 4x400-meter relay team that won gold for the third straight time. Sanya is a well-decorated athlete as well as a successful off-the-track business lady and personality. She spends a lot of her time speaking on behalf of humanitarian issues and is the founder of the Sanya Richards-Ross Fast Track Program in Kingston, Jamaica.

Her speed has brought her many accomplishments. She owes a great deal of her success to being a fast runner. And that has come via talent and hard work. But there are a couple of areas where she takes her time and does not rush through: reading the Bible and talking to God in prayer.

"Prayer is a very important," she told *Sports Spectrum*. "My husband and I pray together every time we're together; at nights before we go to bed, we try to do Bible study together. My best friend and I pray before races. We don't just pray just because of races, but it's something that allows us to come together. It's a commonality that we have. So, prayer is very important to me, it's our direct line to Jesus, and we know that He hears us. Where two or more are gathered, we know that He's there with us (referencing Matthew 18:20), so whenever I can I try to pray with my teammates to encourage them as well."

And what about spending time in the Word of God?

"The Bible is also very important to me," she added. "I think that is where we get all the information that we need to equip us for life. I know last year when I was struggling, I kept reading the book of Job, and all that he went through, and how patient he was and that he never cursed God. I feel like everything we go though in life, there is a reference to it in the Bible, and if we're patient enough and if we're willing to read it, you find that peace and it gives you that resolve that you need to persevere, so the Bible is very important to me as well."

How much time do you spend reading God's Word and in prayer?

> *Teach me your way, O LORD,*
> *that I may walk in your truth;*
> *unite my heart to fear your name.*
> —Psalm 86:11

Put in the Work

Today, being fast is a way of life. You get frustrated if the person in the car in front of you doesn't hit the gas pedal immediately after the light turns green. You get irritated if you wait in line at a fast-food restaurant for more than three minutes. And the news and scores are the same way. You want it NOW. It's a fast-paced society. How are you when it comes to time in prayer with the Lord or reading what He has to say about life in the Bible? Do you whiz through it like running a 400-meter dash? Do you even find time to honor Him in prayer every day? It's easy to get distracted when it comes time for these. But like every other blessing in life, time should never be rushed.

Wear the Medal

Time never stops. How you spend it matters. It's OK to spend it on fun activities like a round of golf or fishing or talking with friends. It's also acceptable to scroll on social media for a bit—but not too long because the devil uses that as a trap and to waste your time otherwise spent with God. How you juggle and manage your time is vital, and how you limit distractions is a full-time job. Here are some tips on how to slow down in order to give God the time He deserves.

1. Prioritize. It's not uncommon to put the things you love in order. You may make it a priority to spend time with family and friends, or you might make that time at the gym a ritual and never miss. But how much time do you allocate for the One who gave His life for you? A good practice is to spend time with the Lord *first* thing in the morning. Put aside everything else for fifteen to twenty minutes and read a chapter in the Word of God and then thank Him for all the blessings in life. You can also do this at night before bed. Whenever you do, make it the first thing or last thing you do in the twenty-four hours He gave you.

2. Limit distractions. Turn off your phone and the television while you read Scripture and pray. You won't miss anything major in life in that time, and you will be encouraged and uplifted when you do this. "Let your eyes look directly forward, and your gaze be straight before you" (Proverbs 4:25).

3. Put it in your calendar. This may sound silly, but you put other important events on your phone or tablet. When you set your alarms, put one down to remind you to read and pray.

4. Journal your thoughts. If it's important to you, then you will find time. One thing you might want to do is make a journal entry each day. That will help you to get into the habit of reading the Bible and praying to God. After each day, take two minutes and write down your thoughts and items for prayer. Go back a few months after and see how God has answered those prayers or

how He has moved in your life. It's a long journey so don't be in a hurry.

5. Take advantage of opportunities. If you have some downtime, put down your phone and stop scrolling and just thank God for His presence in your life. This doesn't have to be a formal prayer or significant amount of time. Just think of how good you feel when a friend tells you how important you are out of the blue. Do the same thing to Christ. He loves those fast moments. The key to success is to do this often. "Commit your work to the LORD, and your plans will be established" (Proverbs 16:3).

Sanya may be fast, but she slows down to take time for what matters the most in her life. You don't have to be a speedster and in a hurry. Take time for God because He has done so much for you. Slow down.

Day 14

WHY NOT YOU?

Jessica Long

By Caris Snider

For you formed my inward parts;
you knitted me together in my mother's womb.
I praise you, for I am fearfully and wonderfully
made.
Wonderful are your works;
my soul knows it very well.

—Psalm 139:13–14

Disability does not get to define her ability in this life. God already did that when He created Jessica Long.

It was in a Siberian orphanage where Jessica's adoptive parents, Steve and Beth Long, found her and knew she was meant to be a part of their family in Baltimore, Maryland. The Longs made the difficult decision to have both of Jessica's lower legs amputated at eighteen months old due to being born without her fibula bones. This would begin her difficult road of going on the surgeon's table twenty-five times.

Being different was not lost on Jessica. She knew she was not like everyone else, but her parents made sure that she knew God had a plan for her. She was not forgotten. Hearing these words did not stop her from feeling angry and wondering why God would make her this way.

She found the beginning phases of His plan in the water. At twelve years of age, Jessica earned a spot on the Paralympic team for the USA. She became the youngest Paralympian to win a gold medal in the 2004 Paralympics in Athens.

Not just one but three gold medals.

Jessica Long has gone on to be in all Paralympics since then with a current medal count of twenty-nine and sixteen of them being gold.

The medals, commercials, and rise in popularity could not fill the emptiness in her heart. In an interview with CBN, Jessica had this to share, "I think I was just tired of being angry. I think I was tired of carrying all this weight. I think, you know, nothing was still satisfying my soul, and that's all I'd ever heard my whole life, right, is God is the One. He's the One that can fulfill and satisfy every—all of your needs."

One evening in the summer of 2013, she stopped running from God and ran to Him at the altar. Releasing all of herself in the arms of Jesus relieved all the weight she had been burdened with for so long.

She was given an opportunity to challenge the students at Liberty University and she left them with this advice: "Why NOT you to have this extraordinary life? Why NOT you to have this amazing, purpose-filled life? And to know that God has always had a plan. Trust me, there was a time when I did not like that line but it is the greatest thing in the world to follow God and to just give your whole heart to Him and to know that He's always had a plan for you and trust Him and lean on Him when things get hard."

> *The counsel of the LORD stands forever,*
> *the plans of his heart to all generations.*
> —Psalm 33:11

Put in the Work

Jessica Long found herself wondering why she was made the way God made her. For a season, anger and unforgiveness pushed her into a place of holding a heavy burden of doubt and lack of identity until she turned toward Jesus. Have you ever found yourself doubting God's plan for your life? Have you ever thought He made a mistake in creating you the way He did? Have you ever been in a place where you were angry with Him?

Wear the Medal

Just as Jessica found relief in the arms of Jesus, you can too. If you have been sensing the call to go deeper with Him, now is the time to jump in! The amazing thing about our heavenly Father is He created each of us with a unique skill set. Apply these next few steps to help you walk out an extraordinary life.

1. Discover what God says. Reading your Bible every day reveals *who* He authentically is and how He views you. Take time in the morning to grow in your relationship

with Jesus. Start with fifteen minutes. Ask the Holy Spirit to guide you and reveal what the Lord wants to show you. Using a devotional or Bible study are great guides to get you started.

2. Speak life. What are the words you use about yourself? Would you use those words to describe a friend? If you are speaking negative things over your life, it is time to delete those and start with new statements! Research who the Bible says you are. Grab a notecard set. Begin writing these fresh declarations down and say them out loud every day. "Death and life are in the power of the tongue, and those who love it will eat its fruits" (Proverbs 18:21).

3. Do the uncommon things. Jessica had to get comfortable being uncomfortable. She knew her body looked different from other swimmers around her, but she had a goal. This mindset led her to the opportunity to train with Michael Phelps. God's plan for you is waiting outside your comfort zone. Start with one step outside of your comfort zone. Don't focus on the result, just get the experience. "He said, 'Come.' So Peter got out of the boat and walked on the water and came to Jesus" (Matthew 14:29).

4. Write it down. Keeping a record of your prayers and God's answers will build your faith muscle. You may have started using a notebook with this devotional book. Begin writing your prayers down and date them. As you see God moving, write down His answer and add the new date.

5. Take some laps. The water might look frightening, but the time has come to dive in. You are needed for such a time as this. Practice these steps and then repeat. There is something only God can do on the other side of your cannonball in!

Just as Jessica asked the Liberty students, I ask you—Why *not* you?

Day 15

YOUR WAKE-UP CALL

Riley Gaines

By Del Duduit

For we do not wrestle against flesh and blood, but against the rulers, against the authorities, against the cosmic powers over this present darkness, against the spiritual forces of evil in the heavenly places.

—Ephesians 6:12

Occasionally, something astounding happens that causes an uproar.

Magnificent events can persuade and influence the most casual person to wake up and get involved and make a difference.

The church sat back in 1962 and watched as the US Supreme Court banned prayer in school. In 1973, religious people did nothing when the same court said a woman had the right to terminate her unborn child. And in 2022, Riley Gaines, a female swimmer from the University of Kentucky, took a stand in a fight that no one saw coming.

During the 200-yard NCAA freestyle championship, the final event of her career, Riley recalled having no choice but to compete against a 6'1" male—Will Thomas. Two years earlier, Will, a swimmer for the University of Pennsylvania, came out as a trans woman named Lia and switched from the male swim team to the female team.

Riley said she and her teammates discovered not only that they would have to compete against a man but also that they and other female competitors would have to undress in the same locker room as Thomas.

Since then, Riley has been on a worldwide crusade to make sure the playing field is level for women. And this fight has brought her closer to God.

"I've always been spiritual. But this past year, I really have been spiritually awakened. I've seen so evidently how God moves through people, how He has His hand on me in this situation, in this fight," Riley said in an interview with the *Christian Post* in 2023.

"But that being said, I've also seen so evidently how His opposition works and moves through people in not the same way."

Riley has been thrust into the national spotlight for defending women in a fight she never wanted. She has testified before the US Congress and sued the NCAA among other activities. Because of that, she has also been attacked for her views. She told *Christian Post* that she takes comfort in her favorite Bible verse, Romans 8:18, "For I consider that the sufferings of this present time are not worth comparing to the glory that is to be

DAY 15: YOUR WAKE-UP CALL

revealed to us." She said she used to relate it to swimming, but it is just as applicable now, in this present fight. She said, "The suffering, which is, of course, the backlash, the emotional toll . . . is so worth it when you understand what's at stake and when you understand what you're fighting for, which is, of course, this next generation."

Is there a Bible verse that speaks to you in your time of need and encouragement?

> *For though we walk in the flesh, we are not waging war according to the flesh. For the weapons of our warfare are not of the flesh but have divine power to destroy strongholds. We destroy arguments and every lofty opinion raised against the knowledge of God, and take every thought captive to obey Christ.*
> —2 Corinthians 10:3–5

Put in the Work

What will it take for you to get involved? How long will you wait before you make your voice heard? Will you sit back and watch injustice take place and complain to your friends? Will you say or think, "How can they do this?" Or will you be the one who steps up and lets your voice be heard without regard to consequences?

Get in the Water

Doing what is right is not popular most of the time. It takes courage and education and determination. Once you defend God and His teachings, you will face opposition that may not be as nice as you'd like. And there may be consequences you never expected.

People you thought were your friends may turn on you. If there is something you need to defend, then here are some ideas of what to do.

1. Head up an educational campaign. Host a meeting with people who share your convictions and develop a public plan on how to meet the opposition head-on.
2. Write letters to the editor or blog or host a podcast. Defend what you believe in and send in your thoughts and opinions for public consumption. Always show love and compassion and back up your opinion with biblical scriptures. Don't drive people away and condemn but show how God can use you in a positive way.
3. Run for office. Step up and toss your hat in the ring for offices such as local boards of education or county offices. Christians should run for office or run the risk of having the will of nonbelievers thrust upon you. "And no wonder, for even Satan disguises himself as an angel of light" (2 Corinthians 11:14).
4. Never back down. You may be persecuted or made fun of by your enemies. Will you be willing to lose your job over your faith? Don't go seeking this or hide your faith, but don't throw it in the face of others. Live your testimony with grace and dignity. In the last days, you will face persecution. Be ready. "The Lord will cause your enemies who rise against you to be defeated before you. They shall come out against you one way and flee before you seven ways" (Deuteronomy 28:7).

5. Pray—but do more. Some Christians host the mentality that people of faith should show love and pray and let God work. Yes and no. David trusted the Lord to take care of him and his people, but David eventually had to throw the stone at Goliath.

Riley never wanted this fight. But she knew she had to stand up for women all over the world. She is a household name now. She may never have wanted this, but she will not back down. She stood up when others would not. You don't have to be in the headlines to take a stand. Just stand up for what is right in the sight of God.

Day 16
TOGETHER IN TRIALS

Jill Bohnet

By Caris Snider

I waited patiently for the LORD;
And He inclined to me,
And heard my cry.
He also brought me up out of a horrible pit,
Out of the miry clay,
And set my feet upon a rock,
And established my steps.

—Psalm 40:1–2 NKJV

It is never good for man to do life alone, and Jill Bohnet experienced the power of team during her time playing volleyball at Louisiana State University.

She started out on the journey of bump, set, spike when she was in sixth grade. This outside hitter eventually landed in the position of libero and defensive specialist in her middle school years, where she thrived. Finding her place with the Tigers allowed her to experience the sport and life with a built-in family free of drama on and off the court. This was a first for her to experience in a team setting.

Jill's comrades during the rallies were also there for the gameday coffee runs and the time of prayer in the locker room. Her assistant coach encouraged her in how to live out her faith during those college years and to look for God in every situation.

In a blog post Jill wrote for the *Female Athlete Mission*, she shares about the trials she faced her freshman year of college. Balancing the hours of practice, academic pressures, and the search for an internship on little sleep became too much for her to bear on her own. A slimy pit brought about supernatural change in her life: "I had invited Jesus into my pit. The pressures were still there, but the stresses they had caused were diminishing. My struggles had not changed, but there was a major difference in my circumstances: Jesus was in my trials alongside me."

> *We are pressed on every side by troubles, but we are not crushed. We are perplexed, but not driven to despair. We are hunted down, but never abandoned by God. We get knocked down, but we are not destroyed.*
>
> —2 Corinthians 4:8–9 NLT

Put in the Work

Jill Bohnet was surrounded by helpful teammates and loving family, but that did not stop the trials of life from happening. Have you ever found yourself in the midst of a melodrama wanting to exit stage right, but there was no way out? Have you ever slipped into a pit wondering if God really would help you out?

Get in the Match

Jill realized by inviting Jesus into her struggles that it didn't stop the trial from taking place, but the stress was no longer overtaking her; God was helping her to overcome it! Perhaps you are in a place of no sleep from the stress of a job situation. Maybe the team you are on is filled with strife. It could be that you are a parent with a prodigal. Whatever the conflict, here is a game plan to help you out of the hole.

1. Weep like Jesus. It is not a weakness to shed tears from time to time. When we hold on to our emotions, they begin to take hold of us. Over time, this can allow despair, anger, and depression to take root. Jesus knew what He was going to do for His friend Lazarus. Even in the midst of knowing the miracle, He allowed the waterworks to come on. Follow His lead and cry. "Jesus wept" (John 11:35).

2. Find a team. Not only did Jill have her volleyball team, but she also found a place in Fellowship of Christian Athletes (FCA). This is a group that meets weekly from middle school to college allowing athletes to grow together in their faith, pursuing excellence with the gifts God has given them. Get involved in a group like this on your campus or take the lead and start your own Bible study at work.

3. Look for the rope. You do not have to claw your way up and out of a slippery slope. God has thrown down

a rope for you. It could be a coworker who has reached out to grab lunch. You may have a fellow believer sitting next to you on the bench looking for an accountability partner. God's rope of hope to you could look more like the prayers of a mentor who will stand in the gap if you ask them. Grab the rope and then start your climb skyward. "Rejoice in hope; be patient in affliction; be persistent in prayer" (Romans 12:12 CSB).

4. Get some sleep. An overstimulated brain is on the verge of an implosion at the most inconvenient moment. It will not wait for you to be home alone, but rather it will happen in the middle of the checkout line or a bad call from the referee. If you are getting five hours of sleep or less, your body is sending you a warning signal. Stop and listen. Turn your electronics off an hour before going to bed. Drink hot tea with lavender to calm your body. Look up scripture on sleep to memorize, write it down, and put it under your pillow. "I will both lie down in peace, and sleep; For You alone, O LORD, make me dwell in safety" (Psalm 4:8 NKJV).

5. Do something different. Is God using a situation in your life to shift you into doing a new thing? Change can be hard and scary, but it can be exciting and jaw-dropping to see what God will do! Try something new this week in small ways as you feel God's guidance to something different in a bigger way. Take a new route to work. Order something you have never tried at your favorite restaurant. Sit in an unfamiliar seat at the lunch table.

You are not alone in your trials.

Day 17
YOU ARE MORE THAN . . .

Kaley Mudge

By Del Duduit

The LORD thy God in the midst of thee is mighty;
he will save, he will rejoice over thee with joy;
he will rest in his love, he will joy over thee with
singing.

—Zephaniah 3:17 KJV

Former Florida State University softball star Kaley Mudge always had a relationship with God, but it became clearer to her during her sophomore year in high school. She attended a small group at her church and had her eyes opened to the power of the Word of God.

It was then that she understood the impact God's love letter to the world would have on her life. "My eyes were just really opened as to how I could apply the Word to my own life and how

I could have a relationship with God," she said in an interview with *Sports Spectrum* on the *Set Free* podcast. "And it wasn't just the Bible that I had to read and follow, but it was the Bible that I could read and apply to my own life."

When she arrived on campus as a Seminole, she had an immediate impact and played in twenty-three games. The next season, she appeared in fifty-seven games and was part of the national championship runner-up team in 2021. In 2022, Kaley was selected to the All-ACC first team.

But in 2021, her walk with God solidified even more after she noticed a post on the social media platform now known as X, formerly Twitter. A professional softball player posted, "My result is not my worth." That gave her more freedom in her mind and inspired her to live for Christ without abandon.

"I can go 0-for-3 and the world is not over," she said on the podcast. "It is OK to go through a slump. It is OK to go through hard times. God has my back. God has this plan in store for me."

Gratitude became her motto, and she appreciates how God has her back. "I'm so grateful to be here, and I'm so grateful God has given me the opportunity to be here and given me this space to where I can be the best athlete that I can be, but also be the best daughter in Christ," she said on the podcast. "I feel like it's such a humbling experience to remember that and to not get too far from His love."

What are you judged for?

> *Surely goodness and mercy shall follow me all the days of my life: and I will dwell in the house of the LORD forever.*
>
> —Psalm 23:6 KJV

Put in the Work

Have you ever put in a lot of work just to be overlooked? Have you tried hard to have a personal relationship only to be dumped in the end? Has life dealt you a lousy hand when you have lived the best life you can? Or have you made a mistake, and that is what you are judged for? What about all the good you have done? Does anyone remember that? Why do people only look at your failures?

Get on the Field

Life is not fair. People judge. Others point fingers. Few friends or family will be there to help you when you need it the most. But that is life. You must learn to be there for yourself and others, even when they abandon you. That doesn't seem fair, but that is what the Bible teaches. When you are struggling, here are some ways you can shift your focus away from you and on to God.

1. Redefine failure. A new mindset can be a big difference. Don't look at how society looks at failure. Just because you failed at one thing does not mean you will fail again. A setback is not permanent unless you allow it to be.

2. Acknowledge and accept the setback. It's OK to say you failed at something. Denial only prolongs agony. If your marriage failed, then accept it and move on. If you've been laid off or fired from a job, gather your thoughts and start over.

3. Let go of the negative. The devil wants you to stay in the dugout the entire game. He does not want you to be in

the on-deck circle. He is fine if you never get in the batter's box again. Shut that down and go stretch and get loose and prepare for the next inning. Find the good in the situation or the potential. "Be strong and of a good courage, fear not, nor be afraid of them: for the LORD thy God, he it is that doth go with thee; he will not fail thee, nor forsake thee" (Deuteronomy 31:6 KJV).

4. Let God have control. This is hard. But when you give to the Lord rather than asking Him to take it away, then it gets real. Pray to Christ and give Him your burden. Sometimes if you ask Him to take it away, there is a part of you that still wants to hold on to the issue. Give it to God completely. "Blessed is the man that trusteth in the LORD, and whose hope the LORD is" (Jeremiah 17:7 KJV).

5. Prepare for the win. When you put in the work and prepare your heart and soul, you will win. There is no timetable for God's plan, and that is what makes it special. Your time will arrive. It may not be when you think it should be, but God's timing is perfect. Prepare yourself through prayer, worship, and reading the Bible.

You are more than your failure. You are more than a mistake. You are more than misery. You are more than bitterness. You are a child of God. You will make mistakes, and you will learn from them. Be the clay and allow the Lord to mold you the way He wants you to be.

Day 18

GOD'S PLEASURE

Nicola Olyslagers

By Caris Snider

May the God of hope fill you with all joy and peace in believing, so that by the power of the Holy Spirit you may abound in hope.
—Romans 15:13

"When I run, I feel God's pleasure." This quote from the movie *Chariots of Fire* inspired Nicola Olyslagers during the 2024 Paris Olympics. She took to the screen to find motivation in a true story that happened one hundred years prior in the same city she found herself competing. Nicola walked away with her second silver Olympic medal after she cleared 2 meters in the high jump.

Her warm-up routine caught the curiosity of the world. When the camera would spotlight her, Nicola would be found with her eyes closed, arms spread wide, and a smile on her face as she worshipped and prayed before approaching the jump. After her victory, she told ABC Sport (Australia) that jumping was like being in church. "My worship might not be my singing, it's in my feet jumping over a bar."

Nicola fell in love with track and field sports at a young age, soaring over the high bar since she was eight years old in New South Wales, Australia. She came to know Christ as a high school student. Nicola learned over the years as a fierce competitor to make her relationship with God top priority. Seeking Him first over chasing higher heights would be where she found her fulfillment.

Adversity, setbacks, and comebacks have taught her valuable lessons not just in soaring through the air but moving through life. When she plants her foot to jump six and a half feet over unbending metal, there is a moment of surrender. Nicola must yield control and trust in the One who put her on this international platform, believing He is holding her through it all.

> *And whatever you do, in word or deed, do everything in the name of the Lord Jesus, giving thanks to God the Father through him.*
> —Colossians 3:17

Put in the Work

God renewed Nicola Olyslagers during a time in her life where she found herself chasing results which almost led to burnout. The accolades and numerous achievements were not fulfilling her the way Jesus did. This revival within her spirit brought back to life her passion and purpose in the work she was doing as a high jumper. She realized it was pleasing to God to jump with joy. Do you find yourself on the verge of burnout? Are you chasing results at work, in a relationship, or in a sport, and no matter how far you get, it still leaves you empty? Have you come to the place where you simply want to live in a way that is pleasing to God?

Wear the Medal

Nicola learned that talent and dedication could only get you so far without having your relationship with Christ be number one in life. By getting her priorities in order, this opened the door for joy to come in the work she was doing. Here are some steps you can take to live in God's pleasure.

1. Identify priorities. Acknowledgment has been a big part of the transformation for many of the female athletes we have highlighted so far. Nicola found herself needing to be honest about where her priorities were so she could stop the slide into life fatigue and get back to living the life of fulfillment God had for her. Set a timer, grab some paper and a pen, and make an honest list of your priorities. If you discover your relationship with God is not first, pause and ask for forgiveness and then ask the Holy Spirit to help you make the changes you need to seek Him first daily. "But seek first the kingdom of God and his righteousness, and all these things will be added to you" (Matthew 6:33).

2. Make a playlist. A powerful soundtrack of music can get the body and mind ready to face the biggest obstacles, longest distances, or scariest messes found in your kids' bathroom. Worship songs combine God's presence with focused energy. Get on your favorite music app and create a set list filled with melodies all about Jesus. Have a mix of slow and fast songs to keep on repeat throughout your day.

3. Create a "book of gold." Nicola would use a "book of gold" to keep track of every jump in competition and practice. This notebook would hold Bible verses, thoughts of gratitude, and how she practically approached jumps and changes to make. Start your own notebook of these golden nuggets. Take it with you wherever you go and keep track of how your thoughts are moving, intentional actions you are taking, and where you can make healthy changes.

4. Start a pre-day warm-up. A pregame warm-up gets an athlete ready mentally and physically for the battle they are about to face. Using this same concept, having a pre-day warm-up will help us prepare for whatever may come our way. Get your thoughts moving in the right direction by opening your Bible first thing in the morning. Get your heart pumping through twenty to thirty minutes of exercise. Add in your new playlist to listen to while you get ready for the day!

5. Get back to joy. This sounds so simple. If you find yourself screaming inside, "I'm trying!" you are not alone. Getting back to the joy of what you are doing in life comes first by getting back to seeing you are already valued. God placed a priceless worth on you when He sent Jesus to die for you. This took place long before you could do any works to get His approval. As you set out in your sport, work, or ministry, know it pleases Him for you to walk in the gifts He chose to place in you. Keep your focus on doing these things out of a love to please Him.

Don't settle for a joyless life. Take these steps to move into joyFULL.

Day 19

YOU JUST HAVE TO WANT IT

Chantelle Anderson

By Del Duduit

For God so loved the world, that he gave his only Son, that whoever believes in him should not perish but have eternal life.

—John 3:16

Can you lead someone to the Lord?

That's a bold question, but how would you respond if someone asked you how to have a personal relationship with Jesus Christ? Could you tell them why they need to be a Christian? If you are not sure how you would answer, then this chapter is for you.

Zach Rance posed that scenario to former WNBA player Chantelle Anderson, who was drafted by the Sacramento Monarchs in 2003 and also played for the San Antonio Silver Stars until 2007. In 2020, Rance interviewed Chantelle on the show *Life Coach Zach*. Here was the question he posed to Chantelle during the interview. He was transparent and honest.

"I do believe in God. I love God. I see God in myself and in the birds, in trees and in the ocean and I see it in the people fighting for humanity in general," he said. "But how does someone like me, and I don't want to assume anything, but Jesus isn't someone who doesn't play a part in my life. I'm just going to be honest and transparent. How do I become more faithful and how do I have a relationship with Jesus if that's something that I wanted and why is it something that I would want in my life?"

What a question! What an opportunity!

Here is part of her answer.

"I grew up in church," she said. "I looked around me and I saw people who looked like they had these amazing relationships with God, but similar to you, like I just didn't feel it, you know? I don't feel this and I'm not going to be fake. So, I left, and I went and I did life on my own and you know what I realized in coming back to the faith after years and years (that's a much longer story for another day), but what I realized was I had been in the church, but I hadn't been in the Bible. When we look for the church to fulfill a role that God Himself can only fulfill, we're making the church our idol. So sometimes we can go to church and even we can talk to other people about our relationship with God, but we haven't really gotten deep into His word and the Bible, even if you don't believe it, the Bible isn't just a normal book. It changes your heart. I didn't believe it when I started reading it, but it changed the way I looked at things and eventually I fell in love with the author. And so I would say just start reading the Bible. The best place to start is the Gospel of John because John was the closest apostle to Jesus and when you're getting to know anyone you want to get to know their heart and John talks a lot about Jesus's heart. So read the Gospel of John and really get to know who Jesus was. How you would have a relationship with Him and why you would want to have a relationship with Him is because of who He was. The fact that He loves you unconditionally, He died for you. He wants a relationship with you regardless of anything that you have done or continue to do on a daily basis. So that's why. You know? Like that's the best news ever. We search for that approval and that love from so many other places. I know I've looked for it in my relationships, in my career, in my self-actualization, in journaling and meditation, all these things and it's like I already have that love from Jesus. I just have to choose Him back, you know?"

Boom!

Could you explain it like that?

> *No one can come to me unless the Father who sent me draws him. And I will raise him up on the last day.*
>
> —John 6:44

Put in the Work

Are you prepared to answer a direct question like the one Rance posed to Chantelle? Are you ready to be an instant witness? Can you tell someone why they should live for Christ? You can probably tell them your fantasy team in an instant or last night's score from your favorite team. But how are you under pressure if someone is looking for a reason to follow Christ?

Get on the Court

These questions don't pop up every day, but are you ready in case they present themselves to you? Are you strong enough in your faith to share a reason why someone needs to be a believer? Are you practiced up and ready to go in the game if you are tossed in that situation? Here are some ways to be game-ready when called off the bench to share the gospel. Let them know:

1. God loves them. You are not an accident and did not happen as a result of a big bang. God created you. He loves you. "But God shows his love for us in that while we were still sinners, Christ died for us" (Romans 5:8).

2. Sin separated us from Him. Sin is a choice that separates us from God. It started with Adam and Eve and continues today. Everyone is a sinner, and you have fallen short of that standard God has for you.

3. God paid our debt of sin. As a result, God sent His only Son to die for you so that you can live forever, if you've accepted the sacrifice. Your sacrifice is to give up the ways of the world and follow Him.

4. God allowed Jesus to die for you and then raised Him from the dead. You must describe how Christ was raised from the dead after three days in the tomb to conquer hell, death, and the grave. There is life after this and the choice is up to you. "So Christ, having been offered once to bear the sins of many, will appear a second time, not to deal with sin but to save those who are eagerly waiting for him" (Hebrews 9:28).

5. The only way to heaven is through salvation. God prepared a place for you to go after this life. He wants you to be with Him forever, but that decision is yours alone. No one can make it for you.

You can be prepared to be a witness for Christ as long as you study the Word of God, attend church on a regular basis, and pray every day. It takes practice, and just like any successful athlete, you must want to be good.

Day 20
WHEN STRUGGLES ARE BEST

Sabrina Ionescu

By Caris Snider

Not only that, but we rejoice in our sufferings, knowing that suffering produces endurance, and endurance produces character, and character produces hope, and hope does not put us to shame, because God's love has been poured into our hearts through the Holy Spirit who has been given to us.

—Romans 5:3–5

The struggle was real for Sabrina Ionescu looking for a place to play a sport she loved. She was bouncing a basketball in her driveway at three years old. There was no special gym or trainer for this eager athlete raised in California. The concrete courts of the park with her twin brother, Eddy, and her older brother Andrei's ten-foot hoop became her teachers.

Sabrina's middle school did not have a girls' team so she would be prepared with basketball shoes in hand just in case the opportunity came for her to play on the boys' team. Her brother Eddy recalled one game when they had only four players warming up. He told an interviewer with ESPN, "I asked my coach if it was all right to have my sister play with us. At first, he was a little skeptical. She absolutely killed it that game. If we ever needed a player, I would just look at Sabrina."

By the time she entered high school, Sabrina was making a name for herself. Even though she was considered small, her competitive drive left no doubt what kind of player she would be. But even great players face heartbreaking moments. During a playoff game, with 2.6 seconds left, Sabrina found herself on the free-throw line. A one-and-one to tie and possibly win the game was in her hands. She missed, leaving in tears but heading back to the gym as soon as the game was over.

These early struggles became a powerful force in helping her build a relentless attitude to never give up no matter what she faced.

Her Romanian parents made sure that prayer was a centerpiece for their family. Sabrina took this priority with her to Oregon and prayed with her teammates before every game with a desire to have Christ live through her.

COVID-19 kept her team from having the opportunity to go for a national championship run and to experience hearing her name in a live setting as the first pick of the draft to the New York Liberty.

The Liberty found themselves in the championship series

against the Minnesota Lynx in 2024. The Liberty had to persevere through a difficult game three. They were not going to be satisfied with almost winning. Sabrina had the ball in her hands behind the three-point line with seven seconds to go, and this time, she made it. Sabrina's team would go on to win the first championship for the New York Liberty.

The struggles she encountered throughout her life prepared her for the big moment.

> *Fear not, for I am with you;*
> *be not dismayed, for I am your God;*
> *I will strengthen you, I will help you,*
> *I will uphold you with my righteous right*
> *hand.*
>
> —Isaiah 41:10

Put in the Work

Sabrina refused to be stopped by any obstacle she faced. She chose to use the interference as an opportunity to break through instead of breaking down. What is hindering you from competing in your life? Has the enemy's pursuit to kill, steal, and destroy everything around you brought you to a place where enough is enough?

Get on the Court

It can be so easy for us to see struggles as a setback instead of a setup for something great. You may find yourself in a challenging situation thinking you have done something wrong when it is actually God taking you through a holy refining. Here are actions you can put into place to go through the fire and come forth as gold.

1. Put your foot down. No longer allow the voice of a bully in your head to stop you. Instead of being your biggest critic, be your biggest fan. Stomp out the lies of the enemy wanting to hold you back. Take your thoughts captive by thinking about what you are thinking about. If it does not line up with God's Word, put your foot down and don't let it take root. Practice saying out loud life-giving statements. "We destroy arguments and every lofty opinion raised against the knowledge of God, and take every thought captive to obey Christ" (2 Corinthians 10:5).

2. Change your circle. Sabrina surrounded herself with those who would make her better. She had to compete harder against her brothers, but those early clashes prepared her to be victorious in battles to come. If your circle is not challenging you to grow in your walk with Christ, find a new circle. When the moments of wrestling come, you will want to be ready to stand firm. Having friends around you who will champion you to grow in your walk with Christ will link arms with you so that you are not alone in the fire.

3. Pray and pray again. It can be easy to overlook this simple practice. Prayer changes things. We can see throughout Scripture how prayer moved the heart of God. Jesus instructs us to pray in all situations. Staying in this constant state of talking to the Lord doesn't have to be long and drawn out. Short, sweet, and filled with childlike faith is all you need.

4. Embrace the struggle. God's holy, refining fire is burning off everything you don't need. He is using it to

reveal more of who He is and how you can depend on Him. Keep walking through the flames. They will not scorch you. When you get to the other side, you will see it was worth it not to avoid the process God needed to take you through. "But he knows the way that I take; when he has tried me, I shall come out as gold" (Job 23:10).

5. Celebrate the victory. There is nothing wrong in celebrating the win! This step will be difficult for some of you. The anxieties of wondering if something bad will be right around the corner can feel restricting. Give yourself twenty-four hours to relish in the achievement. Turn on your favorite praise music, get out your gratitude journal, and take time to give God the glory. Reach out to your circle and enjoy the moment together through a group text or at your favorite meeting spot.

No matter when the struggle comes on the court, on the job, or somewhere else, welcome it with open arms knowing that God has what is best for you on the other side!

Day 21
YOU DON'T HAVE TO IMAGINE

Tobin Heath

By Del Duduit

Proclaiming the kingdom of God and teaching about the Lord Jesus Christ with all boldness and without hindrance.

—Acts 28:31

Tobin Heath has been described as one of the most skilled players in the history of the USA's much-heralded women's soccer program. The forward and midfielder for Team USA from New Jersey, was named the US Soccer Athlete of the Year in 2016 and the US Soccer Young Female Athlete of the Year in 2009.

She helped her team win the gold medal at the 2008 Beijing summer Olympics, the 2012 London summer Olympics, as well as the 2015 FIFA Women's World Cup and the 2019 FIFA

Women's World Cup to name a few. In college, she guided her Tar Heels of North Carolina to three NCAA titles.

Although she thrives in competition, she always gives honor and glory to God in person and on social media, no matter what. "I was fortunate enough to grow up in a Christian home and an awesome family," she told Beliefnet in an interview in 2011. "Our family was just really passionate about Jesus. I had a great experience growing up. Like many kids, I wanted to do my own thing, so it wasn't until around the end of high school and start of college that I started to develop my own faith. I stopped piggybacking off of my family's (faith) and wanted to figure out what it was all about. I got super interested in things and obviously from there it's just grown.

"Like anyone who has a relationship (with Jesus) knows, the coolest thing about it is that it's infinite how much you can learn and begin to understand. It's something that grabbed me."

She never backs down on the field of play or in her public life when it comes to her convictions. She knows God has been good to her and that is why she gives Him glory.

"I can't even imagine going through life without my relationship with Jesus," she added. "So much of it is me relying on Him and me needing Him, not just in those crazy circumstances but in the day-to-day activities."

You don't have to imagine—you can live it every day with confidence.

> *In whom we have boldness and access with confidence through our faith in him.*
>
> —Ephesians 3:12

Put in the Work

You may not have a large platform like Tobin has to share the gospel or to let the world know you love the Lord. You might not compete on the world stage in sports for all to view your success on the field of play and your adoration for the Savior. But you do have influence. It may not be to six hundred thousand people, but it's just as important. Your circle of friends and family sees your success and failure. What else do they see?

Wear the Medal

You can be a light in your community and on the job just as much as Tobin is to soccer and to her followers. Your influence, no matter how big or small, is just as crucial to those around you. When you have a big win, who do you give praise to? Yourself? Your boss? When you fail, who do you blame? God? Life is complicated and filled with pressure. Here are some ways to let everyone see God in you, no matter what happens in your life.

1. Demonstrate joy. You don't have to like a situation to have joy in your heart. If you lose your job, it's OK to be frustrated or irritated. But that doesn't quench the joy you have within Christ. That is what people need to see. They need to see that nothing will take away the joy you have as a Christian because you know how the story ends.

2. Choose words wisely. The devil wants you to blow off at the mouth and say hurtful things when there is tension. You represent the Kingdom of God, and what you say matters. Be careful when you are placed in a difficult

situation with people who are not being so kind with their tongue.

3. Keep your cool. Like the previous point, make it a priority to not lose your temper and throw a fit in front of anyone. You are an ambassador for the Lord, and your actions matter. If you don't agree with the call from an official on the field, let it go. Chances are your words will not change the play, but it can change someone's opinion about you. "Know this, my beloved brothers: let every person be quick to hear, slow to speak, slow to anger; for the anger of man does not produce the righteousness of God" (James 1:19–20).

4. Love those who may be unlovable. Those around you who do not know Christ need to see your love for them more than anyone else. It's easy to love those who love you. But do you make an effort to show love for those who are not popular or who have done something wrong in the eyes of society.

5. Forgive without judgment. If Jesus Christ has forgiven you, then who are you to hold a grudge or place judgment on someone who is just as much of a sinner as you. Forgive. Forget. "Let all bitterness and wrath and anger and clamor and slander be put away from you, along with all malice. Be kind to one another, tenderhearted, forgiving one another, as God in Christ forgave you" (Ephesians 4:31–32).

Tobin said she cannot imagine living a life without Christ. Neither should you. Live life . . . every day.

Day 22

GET UP

Yemisi Ogunleye

By Caris Snider

*For the righteous falls seven times and rises again,
but the wicked stumble in times of calamity.*
—Proverbs 24:16

A fall in the slippery throwing circle brought shot-putter Yemisi Ogunleye into a defining moment during the 2024 Paris Olympic Games. One tumble ushered in a multitude of questions after her first attempt, leaving her with the choice to rise above or throw in the towel.

What would you do if you were faced with a stark situation that brought you to your knees and left you with a life-altering decision? Yemisi chose to get up. On her sixth and final attempt, her throw landed on 20.00 meters. This put her just fourteen centimeters ahead of New Zealand's shot-putter, Maddi Wesche, to win the gold medal for Germany. Courage changed everything for Yemisi.

The medalists came in for their press conference, and no one expected a gospel song to break out. The final question went to Yemisi about her participation in the choir at Christ Gospel City Church back home in Germany. Music has played an important role in the technique Yemisi uses during her shot-put throws, so it should be no surprise that it was a song getting her back up to go do the miraculous.

Yemisi was asked if there had been a certain song she focused on during the competition. She didn't just tell the words; she sang them. Yemisi belted out about God's mercy holding her close, keeping her from letting go. This melodic phrase is a reminder we can all cling to in our own messy throwing circle.

> *The steadfast love of the LORD never ceases;*
>   *his mercies never come to an end;*
> *they are new every morning;*
>   *great is your faithfulness.*
> —Lamentations 3:22–23

Put in the Work

Yemisi had to decide in the moment after falling to be brave and get back up. Her training and technique development were key in making the upward shift, but her faith is what grounded her in perseverance. What does your throwing circle look like right now? Are there some slippery spots that have caused you to find yourself in a position of needing to find the grit to get up?

Wear the Medal

Rising above obstacles can seem impossible at times. Perhaps the hardship that has tripped you up is causing you to doubt and wonder if you can really get back up again. Don't throw in the towel just yet! Here are some techniques you can use to get up.

1. Walk it off. There are times when athletes tweak their ankle or fall in an awkward way. In those situations, you will see them jump up or stand with the help of a teammate and walk around. This purposeful movement helps them to refocus. If you have had a slip in your life, walk it off by bowing your head in a prayer of confession. Ask God to forgive you of whatever sin is holding you back. "I acknowledged my sin to you, / and I did not cover my iniquity; / I said, 'I will confess my transgressions to the LORD,' and you forgave the iniquity of my sin" (Psalm 32:5).

2. Change your technique. Competing in several large competitions revealed to Yemisi Ogunleye that the technique she was using held her back from reaching her full potential. By making the necessary changes, she found herself standing atop the Olympic podium. Take inventory of how you move about your day. Write down where you are spending your time. Look for the time suckers and the time producers. If you find you are spending too much time on social media, give yourself time limits on certain apps, for example. "You were taught, with regard to your former way of life, to put off your old self, which is being corrupted by its deceitful desires; to be made new in the attitude of your minds; and to put on the new self, created to be like God in true righteousness and holiness" (Ephesians 4:22–24 NIV).

3. Let go. Negative thoughts and actions are holding you back. A bleak outlook can cause you to settle for the gloomy circumstances you find yourself in. Get rid of anything that is not helping you to rise to a different standard of living. Let go of your uncooperative beliefs. They do not line up with what God says about you. At the end of every day, write down all the pessimistic outlooks landing in your mind. Throw them away and replace them with faith that God can do immeasurably more! "Now to him who is able to do immeasurably more than all we ask or imagine, according to his power that is at work within us" (Ephesians 3:20 NIV).

4. Sing. Have you ever noticed different types of songs can cause different emotions? God gave us the beautiful gift of music. He tells us to make a joyful noise, not just one on key. Find songs from hymns to the newest worship track to listen to and sing along with. It might be in the shower while you are getting ready for school or in your car on the way home from work. Worship God and watch how your attitude changes!

5. Release. The last step for a shot-putter in their throwing process is to release the shot. They have to let it go and trust in the training they have done to get it as far as possible. Whatever it is you are holding on to is holding you down. It is time to loosen your grip and let go. No more shame. No more condemnation.

Yemisi is not the only one God is holding close. He has you in the palm of His hand. It's time to rise again.

Day 23

THERE IS A BEAUTIFUL PEACE WITH GOD

Tamika Catchings

By Del Duduit

*The LORD make his face to shine upon you and be
gracious to you;
the LORD lift up his countenance upon you and
give you peace.*

—Numbers 6:25–26

In case you need to be reminded, people can be cruel. Words can slice through you like a hot knife through butter. Phrases some people say can cut deep and invite feelings of humiliation and discouragement.

Kids can be the worst when it comes to making their "friends" feel down and hurt. Sometimes the intention is not there, but other times it is a direct hit on purpose. Tamika was a target when she was little.

"Growing up I had a hearing problem," she said in an interview with The Christian Broadcasting Network in 2022. "I had a speech problem. I had to wear glasses. I really didn't like to talk a lot because of my speech problem. People always found a way to make fun of me: the way I talked, the way I looked, my hearing aids being too big and my glasses. There was always something that stood out."

The teasing took its toll, and Tamika looked for some place, any place, to fit in. "I think that what helped me find my niche was obviously finding things where I didn't have to talk. In the classroom I loved learning. I loved reading. Sports period. Basketball, softball, volleyball, track. We did a little bit of everything. That was an area where I knew that if I worked hard enough, I could be better than the next person."

She discovered basketball and put every effort into being the best. But soon, a serious injury put a cloud of doubt over her future. God grabbed her attention and let her know that He alone was enough.

"It wasn't till I got hurt my senior year, when I tore my ACL, and it was an eye-opening experience," she said in the interview. "I put my focus on basketball. Basketball was my life. Every single day I was thinking about it and dreaming about it. When I got hurt it was like, take a step back and figure out where you are going, what direction you are going in. At first it was like, oh my gosh, I am hurt, I am not going to make the WNBA. I worked so hard to get here." But then she took a step back and realized that she didn't do it. "I was like, whoa. I didn't do this. There was no way I can do this. God did this for me."

She knew what God did for her and also knew that He was going to provide. And boy did He ever!

"Peace definitely came from God," she said. "It came from realizing I needed to remove my focus from basketball back to

God. It seems like every single time I have been hurt it has been the same thing. It's been that you get so caught up in what you are doing that you forget to give Him the glory."

To say God blessed her basketball career is an understatement. Tamika is considered one of the all-time best to play the game of basketball.

And through it all, she had peace.

> *For he himself is our peace, who has made us both one and has broken down in his flesh the dividing wall of hostility.*
>
> —Ephesians 2:14

Put in the Work

Have you been on the wrong side of teasing? Were you bullied or made fun of? That can be devastating. It can set you back emotionally and take you down to a low place mentally. Or were you the one making fun of others? If so, why did you do that? Did it make you feel superior to tear someone else down? Or perhaps your children are bullied and afraid to talk in public. Those are very real scenarios.

Get on the Court

What can you do if you are the target of cruel words? It's hard not to let it bother you. When friends say, "Don't let it bother you," they don't really understand. That is hard to do because it does bother you. If this has ever happened to you, here are some ways to focus on God and find peace with Him.

1. Realize being alone at times doesn't make you lonely. Find your peace when you are alone with God. Don't look at it as if you are isolated but view it as a time to grow in His presence. "Great peace have those who love your law; nothing can make them stumble" (Psalm 119:165).

2. Find like-minded friends. Be careful here because you can wander into areas that are traps set by the devil. Misery likes company so be sure you find friends who relate to you but who also share your convictions. Iron sharpens iron and doesn't dull the blade. "Iron sharpens iron, and one man sharpens another" (Proverbs 27:17).

3. Ask God to open doors. You are going through this for a reason. Read His Word and listen for His direction. Ask for clarity and for God to illuminate your path in your time alone. Grow where you are planted. Remember, flowers must go through dirt to bloom. "Ask, and it will be given to you; seek, and you will find; knock, and it will be opened to you" (Matthew 7:7).

4. Find what makes you happy. This can be music, writing, playing an instrument, building something, or being an entrepreneur. Make sure the Lord is there and be happy.

5. Serve others. Even if it's the person making fun of you. Be gracious and love those who use you. This doesn't mean that you are a punching bag but that you are the bigger person who allows Christ to shine through you.

Tamika was bullied and made fun of for characteristics and traits out of her control. But she found her peace with the Lord, who paved her path. You can grow in negative situations. Let God fight the battle and find the peace He has for you.

Day 24

HIDING IN THE SPOTLIGHT

Kelsey Plum

By Caris Snider

Come to me, all of you who are weary and burdened, and I will give you rest. Take my yoke upon you and learn from me, because I am lowly and humble in heart, and you will find rest for your souls.

—Matthew 11:28–29 CSB

Depression and anxiety will come for anyone. It doesn't matter your socioeconomic status, man or woman, young or old, famous or hidden away, these mental-health battles silently attack all over the world.

Kelsey Plum found herself in the fight for her life while under the spotlight at the University of Washington. While she was breaking scoring records on the court, taking her team to a Final

Four appearance and Sweet Sixteen, it wasn't enough to stop the emptiness she felt. She achieved more than one thousand points in her senior year, this feat takes most basketball players their entire career, but she never felt like she was doing enough to achieve the expectations of those around her.

You would think hearing your name announced as the number-one WNBA draft pick would evoke a desire to celebrate. All Kelsey wanted to do after finding herself heading to the San Antonio Stars in 2017 was sleep. She was numb to everything around her. The unrealistic expectations didn't leave because she was struggling.

No one knew the struggles she dealt with every day. Like so many of us, Kelsey felt like she needed to push it down and try harder to do what the world expected of her.

It was an injury to her achilles during a 3x3 game that brought her relief. She shared with ESPN.com, "I think He (God) did it for me to stand still and completely reset the trajectory of the way my life was going. I'm super grateful for it because I feel like without that, I would've just kept living the way that I was living. I wanted to have my identity in something else besides performance. My value comes from my relationship with God and not how many points I could score."

Her relationship with God changed what her focus was on and from where her value came. No longer being driven by pleasing people changed how she played the game of basketball. She found her way back to loving the game. Kelsey and the San Antonio Stars moved to Las Vegas and became the Aces. They have won two back-to-back championships so far. She found her way into the first ever 3x3 USA team for the 2020 Tokyo Olympics, leaving with a gold medal. The Paris Olympics in 2024 also brought her the victory of gold with Team USA.

Kelsey Plum has become a voice to the voiceless in normalizing the mental-health conversation. The work God has done in her has not been wasted. Helping others see the love God has for them will make more impact than any number of points on a stat sheet.

> *The LORD is near to the brokenhearted*
> *and saves the crushed in spirit.*
> —Psalm 34:18

Put in the Work

Kelsey's relationship with God gave her the courage she needed in the darkest time of her life. Her identity became cemented in who God was instead of what she could do. How is your mental health? Are you saying, "I'm good" on the outside, but on the inside, you know you are not OK?

Wear the Medal

A pastor once told me God was not mad at me for my struggle with depression and anxiety. This is true for you. God is not disappointed in you. You have not let Him down. Here are five steps you can take to prioritize your mental health.

1. Take off the mask. You no longer have to hide behind the weight of pretending. If you are not fine, you can admit it. Start with telling God. Lay it all out before Him because He wants to know. You can come to Him on your knees in your bedroom or at the altar of the church. Wherever you are, it is time to reveal the truth.

"God is our refuge and strength, a very present help in trouble" (Psalm 46:1).

2. Remove unrealistic expectations. Do the pressures of social media, social circles, or your own thoughts cause you to strive for perfection? Do you find that no matter how many points you score or key plays you make, it's still not good enough? Put down the unattainable measuring stick you are using! This is leaving no room for God's grace in your life. All God asks of you is to love Him and love others. Serve Him and serve others. If it doesn't line up with these commandments, let it go.

3. Don't do it alone. You were not meant to do life alone. When the mental battle turns up the volume, you need a strong support system to mute the attack. Connect with two to three friends to help you when the load is heavy. Find a counselor and doctor when necessary if the mental battle begins to hinder your ability to move about in your day-to-day life. "Therefore encourage one another and build one another up, just as you are doing" (1 Thessalonians 5:11).

4. Slow down. Your body and brain were never created to go full speed ahead every single day of your life. Kelsey Plum found the pause in her life was exactly what she needed to get back into the right relationship with God. It gave space for healing to happen. No longer fill your time with busyness. Embrace a leisurely pace for a season. Give your mind a divine delay.

5. Prioritize your mental health daily. Working out your body helps to build your muscles and keep your phy-

sique in good shape. This takes an intentional decision to grab the weights and get in the gym. The same is required to get your mental health in the best possible shape. Make prayer a priority. Use your gratitude journal every night before you go to bed. Practice taking deep breaths when anxiety feels increased. Talk to your encouragers. Remove unnecessary stressors. Then, repeat.

You and your mental health matter to God. His hand is out to help pull you up. Receive the help.

Day 25

ARE YOUR EYES OPEN?

Tori Dilfer

By Del Duduit

*Open my eyes, that I may behold
wondrous things out of your law.*
—Psalm 119:18

What will it take to open your eyes to what God has in store for you? For some it doesn't take much. Maybe a new job and location or maybe that perfect relationship to open your eyes. But for others it takes a lot. Perhaps a tragedy or a life-changing event. For Tori Dilfer, it was a series of events that started when she was four years old. That's when her five-year-old brother passed away.

"Going through that was when I first saw faith lived out and saw God work in some awesome ways," she said on His Huddle in 2021. "He provided people in my family's life that not only were there for us, but that pointed us to a comfort so much stronger than anything the world could give us. I saw these people encourage my parents to seek after the Lord like they never had before."

That event had such an impact on Tori that she had the scripture "dry bones awaken" tattooed on her forearm in honor of her brother. She told ESPN in an interview that, "God wakes up dry bones, and that's what He did in my life." The verse is in reference to Ezekiel 37:1–2.

Tori added that God answered prayer in her life when she decided to attend the University of Louisville. When she played at UL, she tied a green ribbon on her shoelace to remember her late brother.

"The biggest way my faith impacts how I play is how grateful I've become for my sport," Tori said in a 2020 interview for *Sports Spectrum*. "Over the past year, God has really reshaped how I think about my sport and how I use my platform. He's shown me that my team is my mission field."

God showed her where she needed to be and caused her to remember to be grateful every day of her life.

"God has opened a door with some of my teammates for discipleship and growing together in our faith walks," she added. "My eyes have been opened to the impact these relationships can have on people's eternities."

What will it take for your eyes to see the greatness of God or what He has in store for you?

> *Do your best to present yourself to God as one approved, a worker who has no need to be ashamed, rightly handling the word of truth.*
> —2 Timothy 2:15

Put in the Work

Are you following the will of God in your life? If you are, that's fantastic and a blessing, and you can skip ahead to the next chapter. But if you are still waiting and praying for His guidance, then read on. When you are in the will of God in your life, you are blessed. At the same time, if you are wondering what He has in store for you, then you can be frustrated and impatient. That's OK. Other than what His will is for you, a bigger question is *how* do you know His will?

Get in the Match

To be in the will of God is one thing. It's a sense of peace and joy. It's a comfort to know that you are obeying and listening to the Lord. This doesn't mean your life is perfect and without problems, but it means you are at peace with your circumstances. But if you are struggling to find His will for you, whether it's a career or location or relationship or ministry, it can be a source of spiritual tension. Here are some ways you can try to uncover what God has in store for you. Some may sound simple or routine, but they really work.

1. Be patient. Don't make things happen. If you take the lead, it will fail in the end. But how do you know if it's in the will of God? You will have peace in your heart and mind, and it will all make sense. "Be still before the LORD and wait patiently for him; / fret not yourself over the one who prospers in his way, / over the man who carries out evil devices!" (Psalm 37:7).

2. Go through doors that open. For example, you may want to attend a particular college or school, but those doors may not open. Instead, you may be accepted by your third or fourth choice. The job you have your eyes set on may not be offered to you, but instead a lower position may be available.

3. Pray for wisdom. Consult with friends or family or your pastor too. Get input from those who have walked your journey. Pray and fast and ask. Be specific when you pray. Ask God to shut doors and illuminate the path He wants for you. "Listen to advice and accept instruction, that you may gain wisdom in the future" (Proverbs 19:20).

4. Prepare yourself. Do this by delving into God's Word and serving others while you wait. This will allow you to grow in your faith.

5. Praise and celebrate. Do this before your prayers are answered and after. God deserves your praise and worship no matter the circumstance. When you lift your hands in praise, He will honor that. But do it out of genuine love and worship and not to expect things to happen in your life. "My lips will shout for joy, / when I sing praises to you; / my soul also, which you have redeemed" (Psalm 71:23).

When you find what God wants for you in your life, you will be excited and content. You have a talent and are special. Be ready to accept anything He wants for you. You may find out when you are twelve years old, or it might be when you are seventy-seven. But when you do, you will have peace like none other. In the meantime, worship Him.

Day 26

EYES UP

Alyssa Brito

By Caris Snider

*Looking unto Jesus, the author and finisher of
our faith, who for the joy that was set before Him
endured the cross, despising the shame, and has
sat down at the right hand of the throne of God.*
—Hebrews 12:2 NKJV

Have you ever had a mantra that you and your team rallied around or that coworkers kept in front of you? Do you remember the impact it brought and the memories you made?

Alyssa Brito, a third baseman with the Oklahoma Sooners softball team, can relate. Two words cemented the vision of the Sooners softball team as they began the 2023 season: Eyes Up. This rally cry took them on an unprecedented journey. Capping the year off with their third consecutive national championship and a 61-1 record, the press was buzzing around how they were able to accomplish such a feat.

Two days before achieving this victory, the team went viral after answering a question from ESPN's Alex Scarborough on how they kept joy in front of them in the midst of the pressure. "I think a huge thing that we've really just latched on to is 'Eyes up,'" Alyssa said as she directed her eyes and index fingers upward. "We're really fixing our eyes on Christ, and that's something where, like they were saying, you can't find a fulfillment in an outcome, whether it's good or bad."

Alyssa and her teammates held on to this sacred message as they moved into the 2024 season. She knew that God had brought her to the University of Oklahoma from Oregon for more than adding wins to their record. Her focus was on using her platform to win souls for Christ. A special moment happened for her when she had the privilege of helping one of her teammates get baptized.

Alyssa and her team would continue in writing this unrivaled story by winning their fourth consecutive national championship. Her career as a Sooner ended with a .395 batting average, 49 home runs, 167 RBIs, and 176 starts out of 188 games. But stats are not where she found her peace. She knew the love God had for her was never about her performance on the infield. "My identity is in Christ. His love is greater than any stats, results, or failures."

> *But in your hearts regard Christ the Lord as holy,*
> *ready at any time to give a defense to anyone who*
> *asks you for a reason for the hope that is in you.*
> —1 Peter 3:15 CSB

Put in the Work

Alyssa's main priority shifting to winning souls first over winning games gave her freedom to compete in softball like never before. The pressure to perform no longer held her back. It was about being a light where He had placed her. Are you ready to get out from under the pressures of the world and move into the peace of living with your eyes on Jesus? Who has God placed you around to shine your light for Him? Do you have a difficult time figuring out how to be a witness for God at work, school, or the sport you play?

Get on the Field

The practice of sharing our faith is scary for many of us. Keeping eternity as our focal point will help us push past the nerves. You never know who needs to see the love of Jesus or hear the testimony He has given you. Here are five steps you can use to practice being a light to the world around you.

1. Don't focus on the results. The good news is you do not have to be the one doing the saving! Jesus took the role of Savior when He came and died on the cross for our sins. All God is asking of you is to be willing to speak boldly on His behalf or use your actions to lead to His love and forgiveness. You can do this in small ways from how you treat people in the hallways to how you talk about your boss behind his or her back. "For God so loved the world, that he gave his only Son, that whoever believes in him should not perish but have eternal life" (John 3:16).

2. Keep your Eyes Up. Alyssa found true fulfillment in her life by keeping her gaze fixed on Jesus. Looking up to Him and not around to the world helped her live with peace and do some incredible things. I know the pull of the world can seem enticing. It can cause you to think you are missing out on so much if you don't follow its whisper. The offer it gives you is fleeting and will never give you what Jesus can. To add this step in, physically look up to the sky every day. Ask Jesus to help you seek Him first and to remind you of His love and grace.

3. Pray for them by name. Prayer is a powerful tool in your life belt. It can be easy to leave this as a last-ditch effort instead of a first-and-foremost resource. Write down the names of three people you suspect may not be Christian. Put this piece of paper in your Bible to pray over every day until they are saved. Ask God to draw them into His presence. Ask Him to use you to be the light leading them to Jesus.

4. Ask the Holy Spirit to help. As Jesus ascended into heaven, He promised to send the Holy Spirit to be our helper. He came to give us power, boldness, and courage to proclaim the goodness of God. Ask the Holy Spirit to help you be the witness the Lord is calling you to be with your friends, family, or even social media followers who read your posts. "But you will receive power when the Holy Spirit has come upon you, and you will be my witnesses in Jerusalem and in all Judea and Samaria, and to the end of the earth" (Acts 1:8).

5. Practice in your mirror. Practice doesn't make us perfect, but it will make us better. Write down your story

of salvation. Begin with your life before asking Jesus to be your Savior and Lord. Next, share how you came to know Him. Finally, write what your life has been like with Jesus. Read it in the mirror until you get comfortable not needing to read it word for word. Ask God to give you opportunities to share what He has done for you and to have courage to ask others if they are ready to become followers of Christ.

God has you where you are with eternity in mind. Use the field you are playing on to share His good news!

Day 27

THE BEST DAY EVER!

Hailey Van Lith

By Del Duduit

*You keep him in perfect peace
  whose mind is stayed on you,
  because he trusts in you.
Trust in the LORD forever,
  for the LORD GOD is an everlasting rock.*
                        —Isaiah 26:3–4

When you think back on happy days, which ones come to mind? Was it the day you graduated from high school or college? How about the day you finally earned your driver's license? Perhaps a special Christmas Day stands out as spectacular or a birthday celebration that will forever be in your memory. What about the day you met a special person in your life? For some, it may be a wedding day or the birth of a child that stands out.

But what about the day you received Christ as your Savior? For Hailey Van Lith, it was the day she went underwater in baptism.

The point guard from Wenatchee, Washington, who played for the University of Louisville, Louisiana State University, and Texas Christian University, said the best day of her life was when she made a public confession of her Lord Jesus Christ in baptism.

"Best day of my life," she posted in the first of a series of five photos from the baptism in an article in *Sports Spectrum* in 2023. "My greatest success in life is to offer my life to serve Jesus," according to her post on Instagram.

Her social media posts also reference 1 Peter 5:6 which instructs you to "Humble yourselves, therefore, under the mighty hand of God so that at the proper time he may exalt you."

According to the same article, she was asked by reporters where she found her motivation to play at such a high level. After all, she was a two-time First Team All ACC in 2022 and 2023 and named to the ACC All-Freshman team in 2021 as well as a McDonald's All-American in 2020.

"I'll be completely honest—I'm not motivated by external factors," she stated. "I'm motivated by myself, and I always have been. If we would've won the national championship this year, I would've had the same amount of motivation in me and that's just who I am.

"I'm not motivated at all by the fact that they named me honorable mention. I know who I am, and I know what God thinks I am. God doesn't think I'm an honorable mention, I'll tell you that right now. I don't need external motivation. I'm internally motivated."

After all the accolades she's won and those she will achieve, the best day of her life remains the day she was baptized. What a day it must have been indeed.

Have you made a public profession of Christ?

> *Do you not know that all of us who have been baptized into Christ Jesus were baptized into his death? We were buried therefore with him by baptism into death, in order that, just as Christ was raised from the dead by the glory of the Father, we too might walk in newness of life.*
> —Romans 6:3–4

Put in the Work

Perhaps you are a Christian and life is good. You have the normal everyday problems but nothing major in your life has happened yet. Do your family or friends know about your faith? Or are you a kind of closet Christian, who just minds your own business and doesn't bother anyone? If so, you should consider and pray about being baptized. Or perhaps you were baptized as a young child and never understood the meaning of it before. Being baptized does not guarantee you a home in heaven—that's set aside for you if you have given your life to Christ and serve Him daily.

Get on the Court

So why should you get baptized? Life is good, right? Why mess things up? Maybe you are afraid of the water, and that's real. But when you get down to business, every follower of Christ, who is able, should be baptized. Here are some reasons why you should take your Christian experience to the next level.

1. God commands this. If you read Matthew 28, Jesus tells the apostles to "Go therefore and make disciples of all nations, baptizing them in the name of the Father and of the Son and of the Holy Spirit, teaching them to observe all that I have commanded you. And behold, I am with you always, to the end of the age" (vv. 19–20). That is a simple command and should be enough to entice you to be baptized.

2. You identify with Christ. This allows you to begin your journey of faith and officially renounce your life of sin. Does this mean that if you have not been baptized that you are not a Christian? Of course not. But it will invigorate you and inspire you to be closer in your Christian walk. "And Peter said to them, 'Repent and be baptized every one of you in the name of Jesus Christ for the forgiveness of your sins, and you will receive the gift of the Holy Spirit'" (Acts 2:38).

3. You tell everyone you are a Christian. There is strength when you make a public confession and proclamation. You know how you feel when you share your struggles and success with someone? It empowers you and makes you feel like you are not alone. Baptism is the same. When your friends or family or community see you make a confession through baptism, it holds you more accountable.

4. It lifts your faith. This is a big deal because it signifies that baptized individuals aren't alone in renouncing sin and living a life for Christ. They have an entire community to support them and offer them guidance as they deepen their faith and share God's love with others. In

turn, baptized Christians are called on to support members of their church and do good work in society as well. It not only builds you up but helps you encourage others in their walk with Christ.

5. You experience an exhilarating feeling. Just like Hailey described, it will be one of the best days of your life. The strength and support you receive will carry you through the next several weeks and help you be a stronger follower of Christ. The symbolism of going underwater as a sinner and coming out "washed white as snow" is a feeling that will never get old. "For as many of you as were baptized into Christ have put on Christ" (Galatians 3:27).

Hailey described it as the best day of her life. You can have that experience too. And, if you've done it before, then think and pray about doing it again. What harm will it do? It may inspire others. You don't get baptized to be saved. You get baptized *because* you are saved.

Day 28

FIGHT FOR CHRIST

Hannah Hidalgo

By Caris Snider

Fight the good fight of the faith. Take hold of eternal life to which you were called and about which you have made a good confession in the presence of many witnesses.

—1 Timothy 6:12 CSB

The Fighting Irish brought Hannah Hidalgo onto their team not because of her towering size or flashy play. It was her lockdown defense and steady demeanor as a point guard that put Hannah on Coach Ivey's radar for the University of Notre Dame.

Her small stature has never been an excuse to hold back on the court. Starting out in New Jersey with her four brothers at the local rec center, Hannah had to figure out very quickly how to play with grit. Her dad coached and her mom was a referee, so excuses were not allowed. They showed her no mercy. These early battles prepared Hannah for the dogfights she would face as she moved forward in her high school seasons.

This 5'6" point guard graduated high school as the New Jersey Gatorade Player of the Year. When she stepped onto the court in her Notre Dame jersey for the first time against the Goliath of the University of South Carolina, no one expected the freshman to do what she did. Hannah's team did not leave with victory, but she was the story on the highlight reel. Her 31 points, 4 rebounds, and 3 assists were a stepping stone into a storied year. She broke the ACC record for most steals by a freshman in one season with 115.

Despite the injuries and difficulties her team faced, Hannah was determined to win. Her defense helped pull out the win over NC State for the 2024 ACC Championship and will her team to make an appearance in the Sweet Sixteen with just six healthy players. During the press conference after securing this win, Hannah answered a question about what pushes her. "Jesus Christ. Everything I do is to give glory to God. I go out and that is what my fight is for. I fight for Christ. That's the way I am able to give my testimony through basketball."

Hannah's faith keeps her grounded in gratitude as she continues forward in her basketball career. She recognizes that the talent and opportunities all come from God. She acknowledged on an Instagram post that God has her doing things she used to watch on the TV screen.

What does God have you doing you used to only dream of?

> *And God is able to make all grace abound toward you, that you, always having all sufficiency in all*

things, may have an abundance for every good work.

—2 Corinthians 9:8 NKJV

Put in the Work

Hannah did not use being smaller than the competition as a justification to not put in the work. She knew she would have to labor harder than others but putting forth her very best with the skills God gave her left no room for excuses. Are you finding yourself in a circumstance where you have pulled back on your effort because the task appears too difficult to overcome? Is God asking you to get in the fight, but you don't know how to take the next step?

Get on the Court

Hannah Hidalgo's path was not like other point guards. This floor general didn't start out as the top scorer. It was her defense she chose to refine and specialize in. If she wasn't going to score, her opponents were not going to have a chance to get a shot up. She trusted God would give her exactly what she needed just like David did in his battle against Goliath. Here are a few ways you can keep fighting.

1. Lock in. Keep the main thing the main thing. Focus on putting your talents to work for the Lord. This will help block out the distractions of the world. Mute the notifications on your phone. Take a few moments every day to sit in silence and focus your mind on the job in front of you. Write down small goals you would like to accomplish when a new day begins. "Let your eyes look

directly forward, and your gaze be straight before you" (Proverbs 4:25).

2. Put in the work. Take your small goals and break them down a little further. Clarify how you will work on these steps over the next seven days, twenty-one days, and thirty days. Look at the effort you have been putting in and identify where you need to raise the intensity. If fear tries to stop you, remind yourself who gave you the gifts and talents you have. You are honoring God by giving your best. "And whatever you do in word or deed, do all in the name of the Lord Jesus, giving thanks to God the Father through Him" (Colossians 3:17 NKJV).

3. Face the enemy. Jesus makes it very clear that the enemy has come to steal, kill, and destroy in your life. He wants to scare and bully you. No more! Get your swagger back by no longer running from the enemy but making him run from you. God has given us power and authority over Satan. The next time he whispers with scare tactics in your ear, you loudly proclaim he will no longer get the best of you. Memorize Luke 10:19 to vocalize in these moments of attack.

4. Don't panic. Our emotions can seem overpowering at times. They try to take the steering wheel when you need them buckled up in the passenger seat. When you sense an internal uprising, pause and breathe. Get your brain back into rational thinking by using box breathing. Inhale for four seconds, hold the breath for four seconds, exhale through your nose for four seconds, and

then hold your breath one last time for four seconds. Repeat this strategy as often as you need.

5. Make mistakes. We are scared of failing. Mistakes show our humanness and reveal we don't always have it together. The truth is, none of us do! The only way you are going to overcome and get stronger in the fight is to learn through trying different techniques. Identify two new ways to put your skill or gift to work this week. Write down what worked and what did not. Have a good laugh, and try two new strategies until you find which one you thrive in.

We need you in the fight! God has given you a unique skill set. Trust He will give you the weapons you need to overpower your enemy!

Day 29

BE NOTICED

Diana Ordóñez

By Del Duduit

*Do not be conformed to this world, but be
transformed by the renewal of your mind, that by
testing you may discern what is the will of God,
what is good and acceptable and perfect.*
—Romans 12:2

Some people have characteristics that attract people instantly. It may be an intoxicating smile or a unique laugh that becomes a trademark to a personality. Some people may promote a flamboyant wardrobe or have a signature haircut that stands out in a crowd. For Diana Ordóñez, it's her left arm that people notice.

The Mexican American soccer standout has a noticeable tattoo of a dove on her left arm that attracts attention. Also, there is a

Bible verse from 2 Timothy and a cross. It's large, and it symbolizes the baptism of Jesus Christ.

She told NBC Sports that she is "a very religious person and very much trusting God and His plan," she said about her tattoo. "I believe that His strength is what helps me every day and it's just what helped me get to this point to live out my dreams and everything."

According to an article in *Sports Spectrum*, Diana's path to the National Women's Soccer League was untraditional. After being named ACC Offensive Player of the Year as a junior at the University of Virginia, she decided to enter the NWSL draft a year early, having already earned her degree.

She told the *Our Game His Glory* podcast in 2022 that the distance she faced from being far away from home at the University of Virginia forced her to rely on God's grace and strength. "My time at UVA was incredible," she said. "I definitely feel like God led me there. It was really hard at first to move halfway across the country because I'm a really big homebody. ... It was just a leap of faith."

She enjoyed early success and found herself in the spotlight scoring goal after goal. In 2022, she was drafted sixth overall by the North Carolina Courage in the NWSL and broke the rookie scoring record the same year. The next year, she was traded to the Houston Dash along with a third-round draft pick.

In 2023, she was selected to represent Mexico in the 2023 Pan American Games held in Chile, where her team went undefeated to win the gold medal for the first time ever. Diana was a key ingredient to the team's success but deflected the glory to God.

"I want people to know where that comes from because it's not just me," she said on *Our Game His Glory*. "Sure, I work hard, and I do my best, but I very much believe that any success I've had is a direct reflection of the things that God has blessed me with in this life."

When fans see Diana, they notice a brilliant soccer player and also that tattoo that tells the world she loves Jesus.

What do people notice about you?

> *Only let your manner of life be worthy of the gospel of Christ, so that whether I come and see you or am absent, I may hear of you that you are standing firm in one spirit, with one mind striving side by side for the faith of the gospel.*
> —Philippians 1:27

Put in the Work

Are you a noticeable person? What attracts attention to you from others? Do you have a loud voice or a unique walk that lets others know it's you when you walk into a room? Perhaps you have an unmistakable laugh that people find endearing. But do they know you are a child of God first?

Get on the Pitch

First impressions are critical, but not a deal-breaker. Some people can get off on the wrong foot and quickly rebound to let their light shine. That happens. But for the most part, what do others see in you that tells them you love the Lord? It doesn't have to be a larger-than-life tattoo. But it is vital in your Christian journey.

1. You are happy. You don't have to be giggling and laughing out loud to be happy. But you can appear to be

happy in your walk. There will be times of unpleasantness or frustration, but you can be happy knowing God has your situation under control. And happiness is contagious and may solicit questions from others why you are gleeful. That's an open door to tell others. "A joyful heart is good medicine, but a crushed spirit dries up the bones" (Proverbs 17:22).

2. You control your mouth. If you blurt out lousy words or talk dirty in front of others, it will hurt your Christian witness. The tongue can cause a lot of damage so be cautious when you speak. "Death and life are in the power of the tongue, and those who love it will eat its fruits" (Proverbs 18:21).

3. You do not look like the world. Set yourself apart from worldly appearances. You are unique, but you don't have to go with the flow. Be modest in your dress and don't allow the devil to pull you into an embarrassing moment. "For we are his workmanship, created in Christ Jesus for good works, which God prepared beforehand, that we should walk in them" (Ephesians 2:10).

4. You pray. Let others see you pray. This could be before a meal in a restaurant or in public before a major event. Don't do it for show but in sincerity.

5. You tell others. When you do all these things, some people might ask why you pray in public or why you dress the way you do or why you are happy all the time. Take advantage of those moments. Stand out for Christ in all you do.

Diana's tattoo is unique to her. She tells the world she loves Christ and backs it up with a testimony that is rock solid. You can do the same thing. How people see you is important, and they should view you as an ambassador for the Kingdom. Do you do your part?

Day 30

ATHLETE TO ADVOCATE

Allyson Felix

By Caris Snider

My little children, these things I write to you, so that you may not sin. And if anyone sins, we have an Advocate with the Father, Jesus Christ the righteous.

—1 John 2:1 NKJV

Can you recall a moment in your life when you needed help, but nobody lent you their hand? Did you feel as though you were drowning under the struggle, and no one cared to notice?

Before Allyson Felix found herself gliding around the track, she was splashing in the water with her brother and cousins at a water park. They were stuck at the mouth of a lazy river without inner tubes. Wes Felix recalls her determination to be a helper in that scary situation even at eight years old with *FCA Magazine*:

"We look back and there's Allyson with a tube around both arms, a tube around her waist and a tube around her neck," Wes recalled. "[She] was like, 'This is what I need to accomplish. This is what I need to get done.'"

Allyson has made it a priority in her life to model the example of Christ from helping others to giving her very best for 200 meters. She saw this lifestyle modeled by her parents. Her dad was a pastor, and her mom taught elementary school while she grew up in Los Angeles, California. Keeping faith the cornerstone for their family aided Allyson at times when she faced adversity and had no choice but to keep going.

A pregnancy scare with preeclampsia resulted in Allyson having an emergency C-section at thirty-two weeks with her daughter, Camryn. Clinging to God and Philippians 4:6 brought her through this affliction. Praying to her advocate, Jesus, she trusted she could bring everything to Him and He would intercede on her behalf.

She found her way successfully around the track medaling in twenty world championships and five Olympic Games, but standing in the gap for others the way Jesus did for her became the focus of this mom of two.

Allyson made the decision to become an advocate for the moms competing in the 2024 Paris Olympic Games. When she became part of the Athletes Commission of the IOC, she partnered with Pampers and created the first-ever Olympic nursery. She became a voice for the mothers who needed space to care for their infants and not be filled with worry. Just because she retired from running doesn't mean she isn't still running the race. God has put her in a new lane, and she knows the payoff is eternal.

> *Do not be anxious about anything, but in everything by prayer and supplication with thanksgiving let your requests be made known to God.*
>
> —Philippians 4:6

Put in the Work

Allyson's priority has always been to bring glory to God and do things His way. She discovered one of the most impactful ways to do this was through speaking out for those who didn't have the platform to speak up for themselves. How has God put you in a position to act on behalf of others? Are you sensing the Holy Spirit nudging you to help the younger generation?

Wear the Medal

Allyson used her life experience to open her eyes to where she could serve others. She used her difficult pregnancy and delivery as her passion point. Allyson could relate to the up-and-coming female athletes who were moms or going to be one day. This gave her the starting point she needed to begin her advocacy journey. Here are simple steps you can take to live as a servant to those around you.

1. Find your passion. Do you love working with children? Are you fond of sitting with the older generation who doesn't have any family close by? Perhaps you like building and working outdoors? Serving in areas you love will put a bigger fire in your belly. Write down what you enjoy to figure out your starting point. "For

even the Son of Man did not come to be served, but to serve, and to give His life a ransom for many" (Mark 10:45 NKJV).

2. Listen to young children read. Classrooms all across the world need all hands on deck when it comes to literacy for our children. Teachers are struggling to find the time they need to serve those children deficient in reading because of the unrealistic expectations placed on them by higher-ups. Volunteer at your local primary and elementary schools to listen to children read once a week. Encourage them with every opportunity. You may be the only life-speaking voice they hear.

3. Find a local nonprofit. The wonderful thing about nonprofits is they always need help. Charity work can go back to the passions you discover. God has given you a heart for something. Look into a charity or ministry at your church where you can put to use the skill set He has given you. "As each has received a gift, use it to serve one another, as good stewards of God's varied grace" (1 Peter 4:10).

4. Write a letter to local government. Jesus stood up for the marginalized. He would often be seen with those considered less than, dirty, and sinners. He spoke up on their behalf when rocks were ready to be thrown. Use your voice for those in your community who need someone to fight for them. If there is a group of people, a local church about to lose their building, or students at your school being mistreated, take the opportunity to let the proper officials know. If a letter doesn't get a

response, find out when the next meeting will be and attend.

5. Let others help you. This step may be harder than any other one. It may be that you are the one needing someone to stand in the gap on your behalf. Humble yourself and receive the help. God has placed those people in your life to be a load bearer. He will give you the opportunity to return the favor. "A man of many companions may come to ruin, / but there is a friend who sticks closer than a brother" (Proverbs 18:24).

How will you step up to the challenge this week? Follow the example of Jesus and look for ways to be selfless. You never know where it will lead.

Day 31

GOD NOTICES YOU WHEN OTHERS MAY NOT

Michelle Moultrie

By Del Duduit

So don't throw away your confidence, which has a great reward. For you need endurance, so that after you have done God's will, you may receive what was promised.
—Hebrews 10:35–36 HCSB

No one paid attention to her, but she had skills. Michelle Moultrie was a softball sensation, but no colleges noticed her. She believed in herself and knew God had plans for her.

She walked on at the University of Florida and went on to make one First-Team All-SEC honors and two Second-Team All-SEC awards. Michelle was named the SEC Player of the Year in 2012.

She's been a member of the United States women's softball

team since 2011 and played in the 2020 summer Olympics where she helped her team win a silver medal. And to think that no one noticed her softball skills before that.

When she was a freshman in Gainesville, Florida, she struggled with her identity and with the direction God wanted in her life. She wrote in SportGoMag in 2019 that she held on to the verse Isaiah 43:7, where we are told, "Everyone who is called by my name, / whom I created for my glory, / whom I formed and made."

"From that point on I'm always trying to find ways to be a light to others in softball," she wrote. "This has nothing to do with my success as a player, but it does have to do with what kind of a teammate and person I am."

She let her light shine and even chose an upbeat Christian song as her "walk-up" song, played when batters approach the plate to hit.

"It's not typical, but it's true to who I am," she continued. "I've had people come up to me and say that this meant a lot to them. This is only one of the many small ways we can choose to glorify God in our lives and sport."

And through it all, the ups and downs of being a college and professional softball player, she remained true to the Lord.

"There have been so many things throughout my softball career that are unexplainable apart from God," she wrote. "I was never recruited to play in college, and I never pushed myself hard enough to think about playing for the USA team. It was the hand of God pushing me along to put me exactly where He wanted me to be."

God noticed her talents and took on a wonderful journey because she always honored Him.

Does God notice you? Of course He does. But what if others don't?

> *For it was You who created my inward parts;*
> *You knit me together in my mother's womb.*
> *I will praise You*
> *because I have been remarkably and wonderfully*
>   *made.*
> *Your works are wonderful,*
> *and I know this very well.*
> —Psalm 139:13–14 HCSB

Wear the Medal

Have you ever felt unnoticed? Perhaps you know you are talented and blessed, but no one takes note. Maybe you keep getting passed over on the job by others who are less qualified, or your social life is stagnant even though you are trying to be noticed. Loneliness can be real, and it can hurt. Maybe you like being under the radar, but recognition is also important.

Get on the Field

God wants you to be humble, yet He wants you to have confidence in Him. That can be confusing at times. Trying to balance humility with credence in yourself can be delicate. But it's necessary. You can show belief in yourself and your abilities, like Michelle did when she walked on at Florida, and be modest at the same time. Here are some ways to do that.

1. Find a support group. Surround yourself with friends and colleagues who are like-minded. This doesn't mean

you sit around and talk about others in a negative way, but it means to encourage each other. This will help build confidence. You can be confident without being arrogant. "I rejoiced in the Lord greatly that once again you renewed your care for me. . . . You did well by sharing with me in my hardship" (Philippians 4:10, 14 HCSB).

2. Forgive. Now what does this have to do with you being noticed? When you forgive those who have done you wrong, you can enjoy the freedom of God's grace and get on with your life. A grudge can hold you back and dampen your confidence.

3. Practice positive thinking. Be patient with yourself and allow for mistakes and celebrate the victories. Don't compare yourself to others. You are unique and God knows who you are. "Trust in the LORD with all your heart, / and lean not on your own understanding; / in all your ways submit to him, / and he will make your paths straight" (Proverbs 3:5–6 NIV).

4. Get out of your comfort zone. God may open a door for you to go through. Take the risk. Pray about it and don't allow the devil to shut the door. Remember, no team recruited Michelle, and she walked on and played at a high Division I college. She walked through the door.

5. Help others. This is where humility makes the play. Show support and help those in need. Never help someone out of pity but do it to lift them up and show them Christ at the same time. "Based on the gift each one has

received, use it to serve others, as good managers of the varied grace of God. If anyone speaks, it should be as one who speaks God's words; if anyone serves, it should be from the strength God provides, so that God may be glorified through Jesus Christ in everything" (1 Peter 4:10–11 HCSB).

God notices you. He wants what is best for you and will reveal it to you when He is ready. In the meantime, take the opportunity to grow as a Christian. And when you do get the "swing-away" sign from the Lord, do it with all your heart.

Day 32

GOD LOVES A COMEBACK STORY

Simone Manuel

By Caris Snider

*And after you have suffered a little while, the
God of all grace, who has called you to his eternal
glory in Christ, will himself restore, confirm,
strengthen, and establish you.*

—1 Peter 5:10

It was a membership to the local 24 Hour Fitness that began Simone Manuel's resurgence in the water. No one swimming laps next to her knew they were freestyling by an Olympic gold medalist.

Simone took the world by surprise in 2016 during the Olympics in Rio. She became the first African American to win an individual medal for swimming. She took home the gold in the women's 100-meter freestyle by tying with Penny Oleksiak from Canada. Simone continued in her medal streak, leaving the games with two more silver medals; one for the 4x100-meter medley and the other in the 50-meter freestyle.

Simone's drive to continue forward for the next Olympic Games in Tokyo was quickly put into Park. She knew something was not physically right during her training, and doctors discovered she had a condition called Overtraining Syndrome. Her speed, agility, and flowing movement through the water was gone.

The physical ability may have left her for a time, but Simone's determination to get back in the water was still there. She had unfinished business to take care of.

Starting small in that local pool was a humbling task. She was not only swimming through the ripples of the water, but she had to move through the ripples of fear and doubt. The courageous spirit God had given her pushed Simone through every rep.

The Paris Olympics in 2024 was her target, and her new coach, Bob Bowman, had a grueling plan to get her back in competition shape. It was up to her to be committed to doing the work and trusting that God would make a way. Even though she had secured a spot on the 4x100 freestyle relay team, her comeback to an individual race was her main focus.

The 50-meter freestyle was her last shot.

She pulled away in the heat securing the winning spot in a time of 24.13 seconds. Simone's message to her fans on the platform X was one filled with inspiration for them and gratitude for what God had done. "I took each hurdle and obstacle in stride. In swimming—battling the tug-of-war between my body and mind and where it was in the current to where it had been at my peak, missing intervals, facing defeat, not being strong, fit enough, finding my love for the sport again, and so much more. In my mind—battling doubts, fears, criticism, questions, and being counted out. Truly, I was walking an unpredictable path, but I saw opportunity. An opportunity to once again, never give up on myself, to never give up on God."

Simone's time in Paris returned her to the podium with her freestyle relay team winning the silver medal with a remarkable finish on her anchor leg. What was meant to be a period in her story, God changed to a semicolon.

> *As for you, you meant evil against me, but God meant it for good, to bring it about that many people should be kept alive, as they are today.*
> —Genesis 50:20

Put in the Work

Simone was counted out by so many. Retirement was thrown in her face. The option of moving forward after her diagnosis to get back on the starting block seemed inconceivable. God always shows up when the odds appear stacked against us to do what only He can! Have you found yourself in a situation like Simone's? Are you ready for the comeback part of your story?

Wear the Medal

The grind Simone put herself through when no one was watching was instrumental in getting her back in shape. The work she put into her mental state had just as much impact as the strokes she took in the pool. Continuing to do your part believing that God will always come through on His end will help you triumph over adversity. Implement these five strategies to use your setback as a comeback.

1. Set an alarm. Notice, I said alarm and not alarms, ha! I know how difficult it can be to roll out from under the warm covers, but movement matters in your redemption chapter. Get yourself up early in the morning to do the exercises you need for recovering from your injury. Use the added time to your day to dream of the possibility of being a business owner, for example, and journal it. Lace up your running shoes when the sun is rising to get those steps in. "In the morning, LORD, you hear my voice; / in the morning I lay my requests before you / and wait expectantly" (Psalm 5:3 NIV).

2. Create a plan with a target. What is your end goal? It doesn't matter if it is earning your starting position back for the varsity team, landing the big client you missed out on a year prior, or running the half marathon you had to put off due to injury. Write down steps you need to take to run through your finish line with perseverance and how you plan to do this every day, week, and month. Be realistic but also push yourself out of your comfort zone on this journey back.

3. Have a goal partner. Simone's coach held her accountable in the training she needed to do to have a redemption story. You cannot do this alone. It is so tempting to walk away when it's hard when no one knows what you are doing. Reach out to one person you know will give tough love and encouragement to help you when the obstacles come. "And let us consider how we may spur

one another on toward love and good deeds" (Hebrews 10:24 NIV).

4. Surrender your plan. Simone Manuel's faith helped her trust in God's plan even when she didn't understand. She refused to give up on Him or on herself even though the road was not well-traveled. Take the plan you have created and submit to God. Ask Him to order your steps and to close and open the doors He knows are best. Wherever He leads you to make a change, trust His guidance and do it.

5. Let go of the past success. Holding on to your past self and previous successes will keep your eyes from looking straight ahead at the victories to come. God wants to do a new work through you, but you have to let go of the old self. Write a letter to your old self. Release all you are holding on to and throw it away. Now, write your new self a letter with a date set one year from now to open it. Tell your new self how proud you are of moving forward in obedience to God's plan and trusting that the outcome is in His hands. Don't forget to open it! "See, I am doing a new thing! / Now it springs up; do you not perceive it? / I am making a way in the wilderness / and streams in the wasteland" (Isaiah 43:19 NIV).

God's Word is filled with impossible comebacks. It's not too late for you!

Day 33

IT'S JUST BETTER

Julie Ertz

By Del Duduit

Delight thyself also in the LORD: and he shall give thee the desires of thine heart.
—Psalm 37:4 KJV

Julie Ertz no longer plays soccer for a living, but when she did she made an impact. She kicked the ball around from 2014 to 2021 and played for the Chicago Red Stars in the National Women's Soccer League and the Angel City Football Club.

Julie was a member of the United States national team for a decade (2013–23), and she played soccer with the Santa Clara University Broncos from 2010 to 2013. After her rookie season with the Red Stars, she was named the NWSL Rookie of the Year. She also helped the USA win titles at the 2015 and 2019 FIFA Women's World Cup. In 2015, she was named to the FIFA

Women's World Cup All-Star Team. And in 2017, she earned the US Soccer Female Player of the Year award and retired in 2023 after the World Cup.

Julie excelled on the field but discovered that her real pleasure came from one source: the Bible. In an article from *Sports Spectrum* in 2020, Julie talked about how reading the Word of God helped her grow as a person and as a Christian. "When I read the Word," she said, "I feel like I have a better understanding of not just how to be a better person, but a better supporter, a better wife, a better friend, and really just see life in a clearer perspective."

She loves the entire book but went on to say this about the first half. "I feel like the Old Testament is so important because it leads up to everything that is about the New Testament. I think that only grows and strengthens your testimony and your understanding of who you want to be," she added.

In 2016, Julie hit a lull in her career and was not happy as a player. She turned to one source. "I'm not going to lie and say I wasn't angry," Julie said in the interview. "It's hard to not be angry at Him. ... I was just angry in a lot of things. And I knew that I shouldn't be. I at least had that at my core where I knew it wasn't right to have that."

Julie said it was the first time she dropped to her knees, overwhelmed and questioning the Lord. It was God who brought her up again. "He showed up when it was important for me," she said, later adding, "I was so grateful to have a basic foundation [of faith]. That's the biggest thing—what are you building it on?"

Great question.

Here is another one.

How does being a Christian make life better?

> *Behold, God is my salvation; I will trust, and not*
> *be afraid: for the LORD JEHOVAH is my strength*
> *and my song; he also is become my salvation.*
> —Isaiah 12:2 KJV

Put in the Work

Life is a journey of ups and downs. There are many high points and low valleys along the way. Just because you call yourself a believer doesn't mean you won't have battles to wage and fight. It means you have One who will fight for you. You still must put in the work to find success. God will not just give you riches beyond measure or a perfect life.

Get on the Pitch

Have you faced serious issues and wondered where God was in your time of struggles? You are not alone. Maybe you've been cast out by family members or fired from your job for unjust reasons. Perhaps you battle sickness or grieve the loss of a loved one. Through it all you must realize God is there and loves you. In case you have forgotten, here are some benefits that come along with being a Christian and ways life is just better.

1. A loving community. Loneliness is real and far too common. If you've been shunned by people you thought loved you, remember you have a church family that should love you no matter what has happened. Fellowship is vital. Find your community and let them love you. "Behold, how good and how pleasant it is for brethren to dwell together in unity" (Psalm 133:1 KJV).

2. You know the right way to live. There is a real benefit to waking up in the morning with a clear conscience. You can help your neighbor without expectations of a payback, or you can bring hope to someone who is in distress. When you live as if you enjoy your life, your attitude will focus back on the real reason: Christ. "Blessed are the merciful: for they shall obtain mercy" (Matthew 5:7).

3. The guilt is gone. When Jesus grants you forgiveness from your sins, you have no weight holding you down. After you have made amends for your wrongs, life will be better. Will everyone forgive you? Maybe not. But that's on them. "There is therefore now no condemnation to them which are in Christ Jesus, who walk not after the flesh, but after the Spirit" (Romans 8:1 KJV).

4. You have hope. This world does not offer hope. It offers misery and lies. Social media will tell you how inadequate you are and that you will never make it in life. But when you have Christ at the center, you have hope. And hope can do a lot. It can propel you in the workforce. It will guide you to help someone in need. And it will leave you with a happy and joyful feeling.

5. You have a promise. Julie was never promised awards for her hard work, but she earned some anyway. God has made and delivered on promises. He promised to never leave you, and He won't. He promised to be there in all the difficult times, and He was (whether you noticed or not). And He has promised you a home in heaven if you have asked Him into your heart and life.

DAY 33: IT'S JUST BETTER

Julie found all these traits and more in the Word of God. The Bible is not there to sit on your desk or coffee table. It was written to inspire you to live the life of goodness and prosperity. She found it to be a comfort and that's how living the Christian life will be.

Day 34

DRIVE ON

Ally McDonald Ewing

By Caris Snider

But as for you, be strong and do not give up, for your work will be rewarded.
—2 Chronicles 15:7 NIV

Her typical Wednesday night did not go as usual. Ally McDonald Ewing received a call from her doctor in 2017. After routine blood work, they discovered she had type 1 diabetes. Ally had just qualified to be on the LPGA Tour. The timing of this news felt devastating.

Ally's golf career began at ten years of age in Fulton, Mississippi. The accolades piled high for her from winning the Mississippi State Amateur twice to being an All-American at Mississippi State University to then being on the winning team for the 2014 USA Curtis Cup.

She went pro in 2015 and continued to experience all the highs of a thriving career.

Shocked by the diagnosis of type 1 diabetes, Ally was no longer landing on the easy fairways of life. She had found herself stuck in a bunker. Ally leaned on her faith, and God helped her navigate this new course she was walking.

She would not walk it alone.

Later on that year, Charlie Ewing would be hired as an assistant coach for the Mississippi State golf team. Ally spent quite a bit of time practicing on their campus preparing for upcoming tournaments. Their paths crossed and wedding vows would come in 2020.

Wading through the shutdowns and cancellations of golf events due to COVID-19, her season that year was abbreviated. The LPGA Drive On Championship became a highlight. The final round would end on her birthday, October 25. She found a way to hang on to the lead and walk away with an LPGA trophy in her hands.

Ally's relationship with Christ, which began at the age of eight, steered her through the surprises of life. Staying connected to Him took her focus off of temporary trophies and placed it on treasures stored in heaven.

> *Don't store up for yourselves treasures on earth, where moth and rust destroy and where thieves break in and steal. But store up for yourselves treasures in heaven, where neither moth nor rust destroys, and where thieves don't break in and steal.*
>
> —Matthew 6:19–20 CSB

Put in the Work

The message behind the Drive On LPGA Championship was one Ally could get behind. Helping the younger generation learn that even in setbacks of life from a scary medical diagnosis, losing a job, or failing a math test, you can drive on and keep going. What setbacks are you facing? How is your relationship with God helping you to keep going?

Get on the Course

Once the initial shock wave has passed, you can begin to realize what you are facing at this moment will not last forever. Making changes to get you through the difficulties will bring about quality adjustments for the rest of your life. Here are five truths you can hold on to as you drive on to bring glory to God.

1. God is always with you. One powerful promise repeated in the Old and New Testaments is that He will never leave or forsake us. Perhaps a financial catastrophe has hit your bank account. A season-ending injury has come out of nowhere as you prepare this last year of high school to earn a scholarship. Maybe the company you have worked with for years is moving states and you have to leave friends who have been your family. Whatever the challenge, God promises to be right there with you. Take courage. Be content. Calm your soul with this covenant truth: "Be strong and of good courage, do not fear nor be afraid of them; for the LORD your God, He is the One who goes with you. He will not leave you nor forsake you" (Deuteronomy 31:6 NKJV).

2. The Holy Spirit will convict, not condemn. Jesus told us He did not come into the world to condemn us, but to save us. He did promise to leave a helper. How will you know the difference between conviction and condemnation? The Holy Spirit convicts when there are thoughts, actions, or words that are not pleasing to God. His job is to help us turn away from sin and live in righteousness. Condemnation will come through a bullying voice filled with echoes of guilt and worthlessness. Satan will use this tactic to hold you back, while the Holy Spirit convicts to help you make necessary changes to move toward Jesus. The Lord will never use shaming words to berate or belittle you. "And when he comes, he will convict the world concerning sin and righteousness and judgment" (John 16:8).

3. Jesus gets it. We have a Savior who understands every hurt and heartache. He knows what it is like to be left all alone. Jesus understands going through physical pain. He can relate to hunger and finding a place to sleep at night. Jesus experienced human weakness and temptation but was able to withstand the attacks. We can be vulnerable with Him in challenging times. He has the answer to drive through them and not concede. "For we do not have a high priest who is unable to sympathize with our weaknesses, but one who in every respect has been tempted as we are, yet without sin. Let us then with confidence draw near to the throne of grace, that we may receive mercy and find grace to help in time of need" (Hebrews 4:15–16).

4. The Bible is living and active. God's Word does not fail. It is overflowing with action-packed directives. Peace brims in every turn of the page. Potent reminders of who we are in Christ can fill every day of our lives. Crack open the pages and discover another level of God's character. "For the word of God is living and active, sharper than any two-edged sword, piercing to the division of soul and of spirit, of joints and of marrow, and discerning the thoughts and intentions of the heart" (Hebrews 4:12).

5. Armor up. The devil is looking to scheme against you. Paul reminds us our battle is not against flesh and blood but evil principalities of this world. To be prepared for these attacks, you need your armor. Write down Ephesians 6:10–18 and read it over yourself and your family every day. "Therefore take up the whole armor of God, that you may be able to withstand in the evil day, and having done all, to stand firm" (Ephesians 6:13).

Ally may have retired from the game of golf, but she still has plenty of rounds to go in living her life for Christ. When the trials and tribulations come, don't cease your play. Take a mulligan and drive on.

Day 35

THAT'S WHY IT HAPPENED

Anna Hall

By Del Duduit

I cry out to God Most High,
to God who fulfills his purpose for me.
—Psalm 57:2

There are times when you may not understand why something happens to you or a loved one.

Sometimes those circumstances are good, and sometimes they are not so good. For Anna Hall, she experienced mixed emotions when she broke her foot during competition. Why did this happen?

The Highlands Ranch, Colorado, native attended Valor Christian High School and then went on to college at the University of Georgia. After a brief stint there, she transferred to the University of Florida where she captured a national championship medal in the pentathlon and heptathlon.

The pentathlon consists of 100-meter hurdles, the long jump, the shot put, the high jump, and the 800-meter dash. In the heptathlon, competitors participate in the 100-meter hurdles, the high jump, the shot put, the 200-meter dash, the long jump, the 800-meter dash, and the javelin throw. To compete in these means you are an outstanding athlete who is talented and can endure a lot of pain at the same time.

In the 2021 US Olympic Trials, Anna crashed in the 100-meter hurdles and lost her opportunity to compete at the Olympics in Tokyo. But that was not the worst part. She broke her foot in the tumble and spent months in rehab trying to recover.

"The injury was a really big inflection point in my career," she said in an article posted on Olympics.com. "I honestly don't think I would have done what I did last year had I not gotten injured. As much as it hurt and I was so upset and I cried for months and I felt so bad for myself, I really think, honestly, that was God's way of showing me, 'OK, you need to change the way you're looking at track.'"

After the injury and rehabilitation, she excelled. Anna, according to an article in *Sports Spectrum*, established herself as one of the sport's rising young stars. She picked up a bronze medal at last summer's world championships and set a new American record in the pentathlon at the USATF Indoor Track & Field Championships.

Anna says her faith in God has played an important role in her career, specifically after the injury and that she believes God used the experience to change the way she looked at her sport.

"I would say that I'm actually thankful for [the injury]," she continued in the article. "I think it just made last year just a really great story that a lot of other people have told me they were able to relate to ... or that it helped them get through an injury. And so that's been really, really special to me."

Anna didn't know, but God did. And that's all that matters.

> *The Lord is not slow to fulfill his promise as some count slowness, but is patient toward you, not wishing that any should perish, but that all should reach repentance.*
>
> —2 Peter 3:9

Put in the Work

Success is a product of faith and prayer and hard work. It is not guaranteed. And you will run into setbacks in your life you did not see on the track. Change is a constant and is to be expected. You can either crumble and fall apart or adapt, make changes, and work harder. And when you overcome the obstacles, always have a grateful heart and attitude and thank God for His blessings on you.

Wear the Medal

You can make it through tragedy and over life's high hurdles. The Bible offers abundant guidance to help you. But its soothing reassurance is mixed with stern admonition. The Word of God is not an emotional boost or a quick fix. It is a game plan that you need to take with a serious attitude. Here are some ways to look at the hard truths and ways to clear the high hurdles in your life.

1. Be open to criticism. Your feelings can't get hurt all the time. Accept the criticism from others who want to

help you. Medicine seldom tastes good going down but is designed to help. When trials come, humbly receive them as a sign of God's deep favor for you. Anna got through the rehab. And remember what all Job went through? You, too, will make it. "Behold, blessed is the one whom God reproves; therefore despise not the discipline of the Almighty" (Job 5:17).

2. Be bold and claim Christ. What does this have to do with overcoming trials? A lot. If you proclaim the gospel with boldness and are a true ambassador for Christ and His Kingdom, then He will witness for you when it counts. Be of good cheer and courageous. This will help your overall attitude and outlook, and that is half the battle. "For whoever is ashamed of me and of my words in this adulterous and sinful generation, of him will the Son of Man also be ashamed when he comes in the glory of his Father with the holy angels" (Mark 8:38).

3. Run from evil. The devil wants you to stay down and will invite discouragement and depression into your life when you are at the lowest point.

4. Have confidence in your prayers. This is not a guarantee for "things" that you ask for from God, but a direct line to Him. Be thankful when you pray and don't be shy about what you want from Him. Faith will carry you through your darkest times. "And this is the confidence that we have toward him, that if we ask anything according to his will he hears us" (1 John 5:14).

5. Keep working hard. Do good to others and never let the world know your struggles. Refrain from posting your

> gripes on social media, but instead tell everyone how God is going to bring you through this part of your life. Be excited about the climax, even though you don't know the outcome yet. This is not a delusional move or a way to bargain with God. It means you trust Him to take care of you.

Anna didn't understand why she crashed and broke her foot. But she accepted it and worked harder to make it and become stronger. In the end, she looked back and saw it as a blessing. Keep your head up and eyes looking forward to see the rewards of your hard work.

Day 36

NO ONE IS A LOST CAUSE

Maya Moore

By Caris Snider

He has told you, O man, what is good;
*and what does the L*ORD *require of you*
but to do justice, and to love kindness,
and to walk humbly with your God?
—Micah 6:8

Would you walk away from a flourishing career? Would you leave it all with no fanfare? Would you take this risky step on behalf of someone else knowing the result you are seeking might never happen?

Maya Moore stepped away from her prosperous WNBA career with the Minnesota Lynx on February 2, 2019. Her decision left many questioning why she would untie her basketball shoes when everything was going in her favor. Maya wasn't waiting on the approval of others. She knew God was calling her to work in a different court.

Maya has been bouncing a basketball on the hardwood since she was twelve years old. Her mother, Kathryn, was a single parent working hard to provide financially for them and inspire Maya to go for her dreams. Multiple moves around the country meant Maya attended four different middle schools by the time she was in eighth grade.

The constant change in their lives pushed Maya and her mother closer to God. They found that His unchanging love and presence carried them through each turn on the road.

Her stellar high school career at Collins Hill High School in Georgia opened the door to a college season at the University of Connecticut. Maya and her teammates at UConn were unstoppable. Over her four years with the Huskies, she earned three consecutive State Farm Wade Trophy National Player of the Year honors from 2009 to 2011. They walked away with two national championships and four Final Four appearances.

Maya would go on to be the number-one draft pick for the Minnesota Lynx in the 2011 WNBA draft and build a strong franchise. She solidified her impact on this growing league by winning four WNBA championships.

The trajectory of Maya's game plan changed when her great-uncle Hugh Flowers told her about Jonathan Irons. Hugh met Jonathan through his ministry as a choir director at the Missouri State Penitentiary. Jonathan was found guilty of a crime related to a shooting and sentenced to sixty-five years, even after witnesses testified on his behalf that he was somewhere else when it happened and the fingerprints at the crime scene were not his.

Maya began researching his case, praying for him, and

making regular visits with her family to meet with Jonathan. They believed he had been wrongly convicted.

This became Maya's new passion. She didn't want to just talk about being the hands and feet of Jesus . . . she knew she had to act. There are no lost causes in God's eyes, so she took the risky step to fight on his behalf. In an interview with FCA, Maya said, "Turning a blind eye to injustice is the opposite of what the gospel means."

Jonathan's conviction would be overturned. After serving twenty-three years, he was set free on July 1, 2020. Nine days later, he and Maya would marry.

Jesus provides us with the greatest example of being a chain breaker. He would be the first to walk away from everything. To leave eternal perfection for an imperfect people. Jesus knew the path He would embark on would be filled with pain and rejection, but He also knew it was a path of obedience to do the will of the Father. He came to provide us not just justice but mercy and grace . . . two gifts we will never deserve.

> *Behold, my servant whom I have chosen,*
>   *my beloved with whom my soul is well*
>   *pleased.*
> *I will put my Spirit upon him,*
>   *and he will proclaim justice to the Gentiles.*
>   —Matthew 12:18

Put in the Work

Being God's servant was always in the forefront of Maya's actions. She knew her life was meant to be more than putting on a jersey and lighting up the scoreboard. It was to be about putting on His love and being salt and light in her part of the world. How is Jesus guiding you to be His hands and feet?

Get on the Court

God may not be asking you to walk away from a successful career. He could simply be appealing to you to help your neighbor or pause your daily coffee purchase to give that money for a child's lunch money. Choose from one of these five practical actions to serve your community.

1. Do hospital visits. The halls of a hospital can be dark and cold. The loneliness of a quiet room can cause despair to enter the hearts of those who are unable to leave the bed. Taking an hour out of your day to pop in with a smile and a prayer can go a long way.

2. Volunteer to serve at church. Church nurseries are filled with crying babies on Sunday mornings. Youth programs are always looking for adults willing to hang out with teenagers to love and encourage them. The food pantries are always in need of extra hands to stock the shelves and hand out to weekly recipients.

3. Assist foster families. Foster parents sacrifice so much for the children they see suffering. It fills their heart to be a safe place for everyone from babies to teenagers in need of a home. Set up a night out for those parents at your church. Allow them to bring all the kids for some fun and games while they have a date night.

4. Yard sale for nonprofit. Go through your closets, storage unit, and attic. If you haven't needed it in the last

six months, put the item in your sale basket. Keepsakes go in their pile, and trash is taken out. Plan your yard sale and decide which local charity you want to donate your proceeds to.

5. Sit with a discouraged friend. Do you have a friend who has been somewhat quiet lately? Are they spending more time at home than normal? Send them a text and tell them you are coming over with dinner. Give two options and bring their favorite meal. Don't forget dessert!

There are a variety of ways we can be the hands and feet of Jesus. Which will you choose?

Day 37

MAKE IT A PRIORITY

Riley Gaines

By Del Duduit

For this is the love of God, that we keep his commandments. And his commandments are not burdensome.

—1 John 5:3

Former University of Kentucky swimmer and activist for women Riley Gaines is a household name. And not because of her accolades, which are many.

In her first year at UK in 2019, she made the All-SEC Freshman Team as well as the All-SEC Second Team. In 2021, she participated in the NCAA Women's Swimming and Diving Championships and came in second place in the 4x200-yard freestyle relay and seventh in the 200-meter freestyle race. She also made the All-SEC First Team and qualified for the US Olympic

Trials. Riley was the 2022 SEC Women's Swimming and Diving Scholar-Athlete of the Year.

She is known for her advocacy of women's sports, but in 2020 she told the *Sports Spectrum* podcast that her faith became a top priority in 2020. "So, that was, I would say, when my faith became my own, but even looking back now, I still don't think at that time I had a good grasp," she said. "I was kind of going through the motions. Yes, I was listening. Yes, you know, those things when I would attend church, but I don't know if I acted in my day-to-day life like a churchgoer, like a Christian, like someone who embodies Christ and His message."

When she finally realized that her convictions and actions did not gel, she changed—not God.

"And so, that's when I started really spending more time in scripture, reading His word, His gospel, of course, in prayer, spending time with people around me who are strong in their faith, really acting as anchors even still in my life," she added. "I kind of understood this cycle, really, and to know God when you know God, or, I guess, to know God is to love Him."

She confessed that, "When you love Him, you obey Him, and when you obey Him, He reveals Himself to you causing you to know Him more. And it's almost this cycle that I found myself falling into. And it really starts by of course reading scripture and actually knowing and communicating with God."

She made her relationship with the Lord her top priority. Since then, God has opened many doors for her, and she has found her calling.

> *I have chosen the way of faithfulness;*
> *I set your rules before me.*
>
> —Psalm 119:30

Put in the Work

Many Christians can fall into this routine. You wake up and read a chapter of the Bible and maybe read a devotional and have a cup of coffee. Perhaps after a second cup of coffee you say an obligatory prayer and go on with your day. You go to church when you can or when it's convenient and toss some bucks in the offering plate and smile and sing along with the congregation. Does this sound familiar? Do you want more?

Get in the Water

It's easy to get into a spiritual funk, and you may not even know you are in one. Perhaps you are not and that is fantastic. But maybe you can start to keep track of how long you spend in prayer and how long your time with the Lord takes whether it's in the morning or evening. You should never just take up time but make sure the amount of time you do spend is impactful. Here are some ways you can prioritize your time with the Lord and grow as a believer.

1. Put it on your daily calendar. This may sound silly, but it works. You might jot down items you want to accomplish each day. Why not begin it with "devotional time with my heavenly Father?" Or end it the same way?

2. Have a goal to read through the Bible. Keep a chart if you are that type and track where you are each month. Goals are fun, and you can reward yourself with a nice dessert if you meet them. And while you are in the Word, take time to study and get a grasp on what He tells you. If you don't understand parts, it's OK. Consider a Bible

with explanations that will help you understand. If you don't comprehend what He is explaining to you then it's of no help. Dive in and study. "In the beginning was the Word, and the Word was with God, and the Word was God" (John 1:1).

3. Set proper boundaries. Try not to let the world come between you and your relationship. This means not answering text messages or checking email when you are in worship time with Christ. Make God a priority. The tee time on the course can wait until after church.

4. Make a list of priorities. Jot down what's important to you. See where time with God comes on your list. If He is first, then keep Him there; and if He is down the list a bit, then you need to adjust. "But seek first the kingdom of God and his righteousness, and all these things will be added to you" (Matthew 6:33).

5. Limit distractions for quality alone time. The world is a busy and loud place. When you are alone with just you and God, make sure the time you spend is quality time. Lock out the distractions of the world and focus on your time with the Lord. For a few moments, make God your focus and not what's on your to-do list for the day.

When Riley made God her top focus, her life got much better than it already was. Imagine how good your life will be when you put Him at the top of your list. Life is hectic and busy, but the Lord needs to be at the top so you can have an abundant life.

Day 38

FROM THE VAN FLOOR TO OLYMPIC STADIUM

Gabby Douglas

By Caris Snider

*And let us not grow weary of doing good, for in
due season we will reap, if we do not give up.*
—Galatians 6:9

Gabby Douglas had a nightmare start to her Olympic dream. It all began in Virginia on December 31, 1995. Her birth was difficult for her mother and the recovery followed suit. Soon, a move to Oklahoma contributed to this strenuous path.

The Douglas family found themselves without a home of four walls. Their van became their everything. Gabby recounts in an article she wrote for *Guideposts* how there was only one meal they were able to provide for breakfast, lunch, and dinner: peanut butter and jelly sandwiches.

Gabby was experiencing an unknown medical issue, but there

was no insurance or money to ask a doctor for help. This is when her mom called out to the Great Physician to do what only He could do. Gabby and her three siblings often heard the cries from their mom in prayer over anything they encountered.

A move back to Virginia and an opportunity to start gymnastics at six years old ignited a fire in Gabby. The longer she was in the gym, the deeper her desire for this sport grew.

Gabby was competing with the junior national team at fourteen years of age, and she realized she had what it took to compete against the best at the Olympics. She would have to encounter another bump in her path to get to the right coach.

Liang Chow had been at the 2008 Olympics with Shawn Johnson and knew how to coach his athletes for a stage only a few would stand on. Gabby was resolute in her belief that he was the right fit for her. The problem? His gym was located in Des Moines, Iowa. A mere twelve hundred miles away.

Gabby and her siblings prayed God would move in her mom's heart to let her go. Knowing it was going to be difficult to be that far from home, Gabby's mom relented and sent her.

The historical run Gabby made during the 2012 London Olympics almost didn't happen. After a visit from her family for Christmas, a homesick inkling took over. She didn't want them to leave Iowa without her. Gabby was ready to walk away from all the training, from her dream, because the feeling was so overwhelming.

Her family, host family, and coaches wouldn't allow her to yield to the momentary emotions. They spurred her on, and it was worth it!

Her monumental performance earned her the All-Around Gold Medal and the team walked away with the same color. At sixteen, Gabby became the first African American woman to win the all-around title.

The wait for her name to be announced as the all-around winner brought an echo of cheers down to the floor of that Olympic stadium. The only thing Gabby could hear was her mom saying, "God is with you wherever you go."

> *Many are the afflictions of the righteous,*
>   *but the LORD delivers him out of them all.*
>   —Psalm 34:19

Put in the Work

A rough start did not hold back Gabby Douglas. Her mind was fixed on the vision she had plainly set before her eyes. When the limitations introduced roadblocks, it was her faith and prayer pushing her beyond. Do you have a vision for your life? Have you ever written it down?

Wear the Medal

Keeping a thought or idea nestled neatly in our heads is nothing until action is set forth. Writing down the vision takes those seeds of possibility and plants them in fertile soil. God did not give you a dream to keep to yourself. Here is a process to write your vision down and run with it.

1. Write it down. What aspirations has God whispered into your soul? It does not matter how massive or impossible it seems, write it down. This step is not meant to rationalize. If God downloaded it in you, begin with acknowledging the objective He shared. "And the LORD

answered me: / 'Write the vision; / make it plain on tablets, / so he may run who reads it'" (Habakkuk 2:2).

2. Keep it simple. Extravagant words are not needed while putting pen to paper or fingers to keys. Identify important ideas through bullet points. Brainstorm possible steps from beginning to end. Explain application points with words a child would be able to follow. Remember, a rough draft is not the final draft, so you may go through several pieces of paper until you get the vision in its simplest form.

3. Share with others. You are not meant to walk out this vision alone. Simplifying it will allow you to give your sixty-second elevator pitch to bring others on board so they can run alongside you and help formulate the best process. Who is one dreamer you can talk to about the vision God has given you?

4. Get started. Time to execute! It will feel scary. The unknown will play worst-case scenarios in your sleep. *BUT GOD will be with you.* If He planted the seed, and you have done the watering and preparing, you will never know what will happen if you don't take that step of faithful obedience. Adjustments will be needed along the way. Submit the plan to your heavenly Father and get this floor routine started!

5. Be patient. Results will take time. God is never early nor late but always right on time. The slow-motion movements through the unknown will try to trigger an unnecessary acceleration of speed. Don't fall for the lies of anxiousness. Stay steady in God's tempo. This is not

His first time to carry out a vision. He did not bring you this far without knowing every step you need to take until it comes. "For still the vision awaits its appointed time; / it hastens to the end—it will not lie. / If it seems slow, wait for it; / it will surely come; it will not delay" (Habakkuk 2:3).

Ready to write the vision?

Day 39

HE WILL GET YOU THROUGH

Sanya Richards-Ross

By Del Duduit

For God, who said, "Let light shine out of darkness," has shone in our hearts to give the light of the knowledge of the glory of God in the face of Jesus Christ. But we have this treasure in jars of clay, to show that the surpassing power belongs to God and not to us.

—2 Corinthians 4:6–7

Sanya Richards-Ross is a five-time Olympic gold medalist. Some of her accolades include being the 2012 Olympic champion, the 2009 world champion, a 2008 Olympic bronze medalist and a 2005 world silver medalist in track and field.

In 2012, she became the second American woman to win the 400 meters at the Olympic Games and the first American woman to earn multiple global 400-meter titles. She is a well-decorated athlete and has been on the mountaintop.

But she's also been in the lowest of valleys. She penned a book, *Chasing Grace: What the Quarter Mile Has Taught Me About God and Life*, where she revealed she had an abortion.

According to *Sports Illustrated* (SI), who interviewed her about her memoir, she wrote: "The debate of when life begins swirled through my head, and the veil of a child out of wedlock at the prime of my career seemed unbearable. What would my sponsors, my family, my church, and my fans think of me?"

During the interview, according to Premiere Christian News, the now retired athlete said that terminating pregnancies is a widespread issue within female track-and-field. She also claimed pregnancy prevention information was not available.

"The truth is it's an issue that's not really talked about, especially in sports, and a lot of young women have experienced this," she said.

She told SI: "At that time in your life, when you're in college, you don't feel comfortable talking to your mom. So, a lot of the information you get is from your peers. It's going to sound silly to some people but, in our community, people don't want to take the pill because you put water weight on. And then people tell you when you're extremely fit, you can't get pregnant because our [menstrual] cycles are shorter. So, there's a lot of miseducation that happens to young women in college, because we're educating ourselves."

She revealed in her book that abortion "broke" her and wrote: "Abortion would now forever be a part of my life. A scarlet letter I never thought I'd wear." And in that dark valley, she found God to be forgiving and loving to her.

She told *Christianity Today*, "When I was in my valley, in my pit, and I felt so far out of God's grace and had so much guilt and so many negative emotions—which the devil uses to trick us—I realized that nothing can separate us from the love of God," she said. "It's so different from track, where you are chasing for *one* spot. But God just wants us to yearn for him, and that for me is the biggest lesson I learned. I'm just so glad I ran into grace."

Have you been so low you thought you could not be forgiven?

> *For all have sinned and fall short of the glory of God.*
>
> —Romans 3:23

Put in the Work

Sin is sin. It separates you from God. It doesn't matter if you've had an abortion or stolen money or taken God's name in vain or committed adultery. Sin is a sickness, and the Lord is the cure. The devil wants you to stay sick and will use your mind and the judgment of others to condemn you. Society and the church can be a cruel place when you seek redemption or amends. But in the end, it doesn't come down to the opinion of others. It comes down to the grace God offers if you want to accept it and move on with the consequences.

Wear the Medal

How do you come back from a life-changing decision? Maybe you know someone who has done something that the church has labeled "unforgivable." Perhaps you are the one who faces judgment from others when you need redemption and forgiveness. What is little to some may be monumental to others. But when you seek acceptance from others, you may find it a challenge to find. But when you ask the Lord for His forgiveness, He will grant it every time. But He must see change in your life. You cannot use Him as a genie in a bottle. Here are some ways to get back on the track when you've stumbled on your journey.

1. Acknowledge the sin. Take responsibility for your actions. Don't make excuses. You made the decision. There may have been circumstances that prompted you, but in the end, you are the one who made the choice. "For each will have to bear his own load" (Galatians 6:5).

2. Repent of the sin. Tell the Lord and not man the nature of your sin. If people want to know, then they are seeking to gossip. Be cautious who you confide in and what you tell them. Keep your circle tight until you feel it's safe to reveal. Never divulge to hurt people but to help. "If we confess our sins, he is faithful and just to forgive us our sins and to cleanse us from all unrighteousness" (1 John 1:9).

3. Seek forgiveness. Ask God to forgive you and change your behavior. That is the best apology when you and the Lord and others can see a difference.

4. Find a support group. This can be helpful if you have been addicted to something or have done an act where support is needed. Professional therapy is also encouraged.

5. Look up and never back. No matter what you have done, you can come back and move forward. Do not

listen to those people who want to see you fail, and there are folks like that. Be determined to move ahead and disappoint those who want to see you fall. "I have fought the good fight, I have finished the race, I have kept the faith" (2 Timothy 4:7).

Sanya was discouraged and at a low point in her life for her decision to have an abortion. But God used her and her platform to help others in similar circumstances. He can use you. It won't happen overnight. But after God changes your heart and you grow and learn, the hurdles may not seem so high, and you can be a light in the dark world.

Day 40

INSPIRE A GENERATION

Karé Adenegan

By Caris Snider

Jesus answered, "It was not that this man sinned, or his parents, but that the works of God might be displayed in him."

—John 9:3

"Inspire a Generation" was the theme behind the 2012 Paralympic Games in London. The goal was achieved in the eyes of eleven-year-old Karé Adenegan. She witnessed something she never knew existed while she watched on TV.

Wheelchair racing.

Karé was glued to the screen as Hannah Cockroft sped around the track. Hope to participate in a sporting event came alive inside. PE class in her younger years shut down the idea of being able to join in any sort of athletic activity due to her cerebral palsy and fear of her getting hurt. Diplegic cerebral palsy affected the muscles in both her legs. The decision was made in her primary school years to begin using a wheelchair.

Others who looked like her gave a different mindset to Karé. She always wanted to go fast, and now she had a way to achieve this feat. Just a few miles away from her home in Coventry, England, there just happened to be a wheelchair racing group training.

Her days at the Warwick track soon led to Karé bringing the inspiration to the track.

Hard work and big belief paved the way for Karé to be in the chair representing Great Britain during the Rio 2016 Paralympic Games at fifteen years old. Hannah Cockroft had now become her teammate and competition.

Karé Adenegan earned a silver and two bronze medals.

She would go on to compete in the Tokyo 2020 and Paris 2024 Paralympic Games. Her current medal count has moved up quite a bit. Five silver and two bronze medals adorn her trophy case, but one color is missing.

Gold.

Even though Karé trains to win and be the best, she has found freedom in not focusing on the outcome. In an interview with *Premier Christianity*, Karé dives deeper into this faith-filled perspective: "I've learned that it's more about consecrating and surrendering my ambition to God. It's about recognizing God's will and God's plan for my life. There is so much freedom when you let go of the outcome. It doesn't mean that you're going to win everything and always be successful. But it means you can trust the outcome is going to be a good one, because you have faith in a sovereign Father who is working for good in your life."

God's plans for your life are good. Circumstances you find yourself in or physical limitations you may experience are not to punish you. It's time to remove the rotten luck belief and replace it with unshakable faith that His goodness and mercy will follow you all the days of your life.

> *Surely goodness and mercy shall follow me*
>   *all the days of my life,*
> *and I shall dwell in the house of the LORD*
>   *forever.*
>
> —Psalm 23:6

Put in the Work

One person's effort to push past their limitations inspired Karé Adenegan to whiz past hers. This afforded Karé the same opportunity to instill belief in others watching her. Who has God placed under your sphere of influence? How are you using your platform to spark possibility in others?

Wear the Medal

One small action from you can ignite one big step in someone else. God has not equipped you with these abilities for your own accolades. He has knitted you together in this specific way to serve others. Below are five different areas in which you can inspire a generation.

1. School. Yes, you can inspire those who are in your age bracket. God has placed you in those halls, behind those lockers, and in that lunchroom for one person. You never know how a smile or one word of encourage-

ment can change someone's outlook on their life. They may feel unseen, and God uses you to let them know they are not alone. Walk through your school this week with your head up and eyes searching. You will find exactly who the Lord has you looking for. "Kind words are like honey—sweet to the soul and healthy for the body" (Proverbs 16:24 NLT).

2. Work. Coworkers exemplify various personalities. Even the most difficult of the bunch can be shifted out of a negative mindset. Every morning, come in with the intention of bringing hope to every room and cubicle you step into. Pray for everyone by name as you drive to your place of business. Ask God to supply you with the right words and actions at the right time.

3. Social media. You never know who will see your posts or videos on the multiple platforms you frequent. A reel you share about how God changed your life has the potential to reach someone in another state or country needing to know how He can do the same for them. A post of your favorite scripture could inspire a friend to open their Bible for the first time in a long time. Use your social media footprint as a place to spread hope. "For whatever was written in former days was written for our instruction, that through endurance and through the encouragement of the Scriptures we might have hope" (Romans 15:4).

4. Sports. The actions you take on the field or the way you respond to a referee will influence the little eyes watching you from the stands. Children will see how you respond to correction from your coach and how you

treat your teammates. They will pay attention to how your mental game kicks in when mistakes happen. Use your physical ability to point their gaze up to God so they will use their talents to glorify Him. "Whatever you do, work heartily, as for the Lord and not for men" (Colossians 3:23).

5. Church. Inspiration doesn't just happen in the pulpit. You can stir others through a greeting after dropping off a crying toddler. Your creativity behind the screen allows those who are homebound to hear the message. Areas of "unseen" service will make more impact than you can ever imagine.

You are in a position of influence no matter your age or vocation right now. How will you go about bringing transformation in the lives of those around you?

Day 41

JUST FORGIVE

Lolo Jones

By Del Duduit

So if you are offering your gift at the altar and there remember that your brother has something against you, leave your gift there before the altar and go. First be reconciled to your brother, and then come and offer your gift.

—Matthew 5:23–24

You may be called a lot of names for your Christian faith. Some of those words may be positive while some might be nasty. People who appreciate your stance could refer to you as "loyal" or "faithful." Those who may not agree with your position might utter words like "crazy follower" or "Jesus freak." You cannot control what others say about you, nor should you try. All you can do is live the best life possible and have a goal to please the Lord daily.

Lolo Jones, who is a wonderful example of what a female Christian athlete should be, was once labeled a hypocrite for having her picture taken with former professional boxer Floyd Mayweather.

In 2011, Mayweather was sentenced to three months in jail for a domestic violence case involving his ex-girlfriend. According to court records, he also had to pay a $2,500 fine, complete one hundred hours of community service, and attend domestic violence counseling.

But before the picture, Lolo had previously endured criticism when she spoke out against the movie *Fifty Shades of Grey* on X, formerly known as Twitter. She blasted the movie that normalized sadistic sexual behavior and stated on her platform: "Funny how some people think there's nothing wrong with 50 Shades of Grey. God didn't create sex for that purpose. Watch another movie."

She took backlash from those who disagreed with her, which was expected. But soon after, she had a picture taken with Mayweather, and the former track-and-field star took on more criticism. She was called a hypocrite for posing with Mayweather, a convicted domestic violence offender.

In an article in the *Christian Post*, it was reported that some on X posted things like, "So I hear that @lolojones had an issue with 50 shades, which was fictional, yet preaches forgiveness for @FloydMayweather. Hypocrite much?"

But Lolo had the best response ever.

"Incorrect," Lolo responded. "If I were a Christian and didn't preach/practice forgiveness or purity, that actually makes me a hypocrite."

Boom! Mic-drop moment.

She went on to defend her decision to have a picture taken with Mayweather, citing the fact that her father has a history of domestic violence, but she still loves him.

"God's judgment reigns higher," she stated. "So you can ask how can I post a picture with him? And I say, 'if I can't take a picture with him, I guess I should remove the pictures of my dad in my home as well.'"

Lolo gets forgiveness.

She treats people with love and respect because she's been forgiven too.

> *In whom we have redemption, the forgiveness of sins.*
>
> —Colossians 1:14

Put in the Work

Forgiveness sounds easy. But for many, it's a struggle. Forgiveness is a wonderful gift to receive but a hard one to give. Some people tend to hold a grudge and place judgment on the sinner and condemn them. That's easy to do, but it's not biblical. It's not what Jesus taught.

Wear the Medal

How are you when it comes to giving forgiveness? Has someone done something so terrible you find it hard to grant grace? That is understandable. But it also goes against everything Christ stood for. This doesn't mean you have to be best buddies with someone who did something terrible to you or a loved one. But it does mean that you forgive the person for what they did and pray for them to find Jesus. And if they do accept Christ, you should rejoice with them and praise God for the miracle. But if you allow bitterness and resentment to abide in you, that is a recipe for disaster. Here are some reasons why you should not let bitterness into your life.

1. Bitterness will take over, and you won't enjoy the present. Bitterness will spoil your outlook on life. You will focus on the past and neglect what is in front of you. Let it go and give it to the Lord. "See to it that no one fails to obtain the grace of God; that no 'root of bitterness' springs up and causes trouble, and by it many become defiled" (Hebrews 12:15).

2. You become stressed and anxious. Studies show that bitterness will lead to health issues like ulcers, headaches, lack of sleep, depression, and anxiety. The devil wants you this way. Bitterness is a trap he has set for you.

3. You are at spiritual war with what is right. Just remember, you are a sinner and God forgave you. In return, you should forgive too. It may be a struggle at first, but when you grant forgiveness, you will become stronger in your faith. Forgiveness is for the sinner and for you too. "Good sense makes one slow to anger, / and it is his glory to overlook an offense" (Proverbs 19:11).

4. You bring anger into relationships. The last thing you want to do is sabotage a new relationship. If you are angry with someone, it will show. And anger is not a good quality to show to someone you just met. "Be angry and do not sin; do not let the sun go down on your anger" (Ephesians 4:26).

DAY 41: JUST FORGIVE

5. You will lose connections with others. Lolo could have written off her father, but she didn't. She granted forgiveness and loves her father. Everyone makes mistakes and commits sin. And those who don't forgive are sinning as much as the one who seeks forgiveness. You don't want to estrange someone over your obligation to forgive.

Lolo had her picture taken with a man convicted of domestic violence. He paid his debt to society and was starting over. She forgave him the same way she forgave her father, which may have been more difficult. She is a stronger person for that. You can be strong too.

Day 42
BUILDING A SISTERHOOD

Felisha Legette-Jack

By Caris Snider

*For this reason I bow my knees before the Father,
from whom every family in heaven and on earth
is named.*

—Ephesians 3:14–15

Felisha Legette-Jack is relentless in her efforts not only to assemble a team but to create a sisterhood on the bench at Syracuse University.

Her time with the Orange began in a jersey before she was behind the clipboard coaching. Felisha impacted the game from the jump, rallying her team to their first Big East Championship in 1985 as a freshman. Felisha's influence was solidified in the history books when #33 was hoisted to the top of the rafters in 2021. She was the first woman to have her jersey retired.

In an interview with the university, Felisha said, "I hope that when people see my jersey number, they know what it stands for—servanthood, sisterhood, a love for family. No. 33 isn't about me; it's about us. As a student, I played for God, my family, and myself. Syracuse University got the residuals of that. It's made me who I am today."

The objective for her has always been about building the family.

Faith directs Felisha's aim and coaching style. It isn't just about the x's and o's with the women under her tutelage. Fellowship of Christian Athletes attends her practices on a regular basis sharing devotions, praying with the girls, and being another voice to point players toward God.

Felisha is looking to build a connection with them outside of the gym. She knows it is in the trenches of life where relationships are tethered. Sure, they want to win games and be one of the top programs in the country, but after the lights go out on the college years, there has to be more.

It is in her focus to build "the us" part of the program where these ladies realize that Felisha cares about their hearts and their futures. The late-night hangouts and phone calls are invited by Coach Jack. She understands what these girls face as student athletes growing up in a high-pressure atmosphere. Building the sisterhood allows them to not have to figure it out on their own.

Coach Jack experienced this love and support as a player, and it has become part of who she is. She said, "When I came to this institution, I had so many people help me grow. People that didn't look like me and didn't come from the same kind of financial background as me, but they loved me anyway because we were all Orange. That's the message I want to continue to share."

> *And though a man might prevail against one who is alone, two will withstand him—a threefold cord is not quickly broken.*
>
> —Ecclesiastes 4:12

Put in the Work

Coach Jack makes it clear that God will be the leader of her program. She knows our heavenly Father will be her greatest guide at building the family entrusted to her. What does the family dynamic look like for you at home? At church? At school? In your sport? How are you creating an "us" atmosphere?

Get on the Court

God's assignment for you is about serving others who are in your huddle. Keeping faith as your top core value will guide you in this process. Here are five actions you can incorporate to help you build up the "us" on your team.

1. Bible study. Coach Jack created an environment where gathering together around God's Word happened on a consistent basis. This paved the way for discussion to bring a deeper understanding in how to apply scripture to their lives. Get together with your family group. Pick a day and time of the week you can all come together. Decide where you want to start and dive in! "Not neglecting to meet together, as is the habit of some, but encouraging one another, and all the more as you see the Day drawing near" (Hebrews 10:25).

2. Quality time. Your "us" might savor popcorn and candy during a movie night. Perhaps the "us" in your sisterhood enjoys reading and wants to start a monthly book club. It could be that you have a weekly game night with your family over a friendly competition with Uno or holding remotes and racing around the track. Identify what it is your tribe loves to do together and set a schedule to make it happen.

3. Communication. A late-night dish session is just what the soul needs with a bestie or mentor. Talking through a misunderstanding will keep bitterness and unforgiveness from taking root in your family. Asking how you can pray for one another will build trust to keep the lines of communication open. Make this type of communication a priority for all of you to practice in your relationships with one another.

4. Hardships. This is not a step you may have expected on the list, but going through difficulties together will deepen the roots in your "us." Strength will come in how you all overcome the peril you face. Has a key player walked away from your team? Did your parents get a divorce? Have you lost your job and you are the only income for your family? Is the news from the doctor not what you were hoping for? Grow through the adversity together. "A friend loves at all times, / and a brother is born for adversity" (Proverbs 17:17).

5. Goal-setting. A group on a mission is powerful. Talking through the steps of how to get where you want to go, together, will offer multiple viewpoints. Have a Goal Session. Lay out what you are wanting to accomplish

and back out small steps to help you achieve this feat. From a county championship to becoming debt-free as a family, it is possible! Don't forget to include how you will celebrate when you pull it off.

Protect the family. Encourage the family. Fight for the family. God gave you this family. How will you cultivate the connection?

Day 43

TAKE ACTION

Grace Lyons Turk

By Del Duduit

*In the same way, let your light shine before others,
so that they may see your good works and give
glory to your Father who is in heaven.*
—Matthew 5:16

When she played softball for the Oklahoma Sooners, Grace had a huge impact. She helped guide the squad to three consecutive Women's College World Series titles from 2021 to 2023. Grace was a three-time Big 12 Defensive Player of the Year and named the Softball America Defensive Player of the Year in 2023. She was selected First Team All-American in 2022 and Second Team All-American in 2021.

In 2019, she earned All-Big 12 Freshman team honors and was a three-time All-Big 12 selection. Her trademark was defense for the Sooners and left a legacy on the diamond as a fierce competitor. She is proud of her accomplishments on the softball field but wants to be known as a follower of Jesus Christ.

"I grew up in a Christian household but never made my faith my own until the beginning of high school," she told His Huddle in 2022. "It was at that time in my life that I realized I wanted to put action to my faith, and I began to feel a strong passion for the Lord. I started getting involved in Fellowship of Christian Athletes, leading prayers on my high school team and inviting people to church. I truly believe when we take action with our faith, God will use us in new ways that we didn't even realize we could have influence in."

She enjoyed giving her Sooner fans something to cheer about when she played but wanted them to know her more for her witness and testimony. "The biggest impact I hope to have is that people can see Jesus shining through me," she said. "I want to live a consistent life in my faith and also in my sport. While I may not have all the answers, I want to be a resource for teammates to learn about and talk about Jesus whenever they want to. When people see me, I want them to see Jesus."

> *May the God of hope fill you with all joy and peace in believing, so that by the power of the Holy Spirit you may abound in hope.*
> —Romans 15:13

Put in the Work

What do those around you think when they hear your name? That's a tough question. What words will come to mind? Will they think of you as a person who worked all the time? Perhaps your legacy will have positive words. But what if your name is associated with negative names?

Get on the Field

A legacy is important. And the best part is that it is in your control for the most part. You cannot control what lies may be told about you so don't worry about that. Focus on what you can do as a believer to have an impact on others. There are many things you can do that people may see. You can be involved in a civic organization or coach youth sports. You can take action and be involved in local politics or be seen as an encourager at work. But here are some things you can do to leave a lasting legacy in addition to everything else you do.

1. Love those the world deems unlovable. It's easy to show love to those who love you. But what about the ones who are difficult to love? What about the person who stands on a street corner begging? Or what about the individual who comes to church and does not meet the "standards" and looks suspicious? Will you pray with them? Love those who may be "unloved." "Above all, keep loving one another earnestly, since love covers a multitude of sins" (1 Peter 4:8).

2. Forgive without conditions. If someone has done you wrong and made amends, God has commanded you to forgive them. In fact, He tells you to do that no matter the circumstances. They don't have to apologize to you in person—although that makes it easier—for you to forgive. And don't put conditions on your grace. Never

use it as a bargaining chip to get something in return. People will notice that.

3. Be happy in all you do. If you have accepted Christ, then you are free from sin and on your way to heaven. Don't lose sight of that reality. You have a reason to smile and be happy. Let others see that. "The precepts of the LORD are right, / rejoicing the heart; / the commandment of the LORD is pure, / enlightening the eyes" (Psalm 19:8).

4. Demonstrate grace and not judgment. You are a sinner saved by grace. You of all people should never judge someone for their actions.

5. Work behind the scenes. Humility is a lost art. Social media has instilled in you that you need self-promotion. You don't need a spotlight to be an impactful Christian. Instead of taking glory for something you did, deflect the glory to Him. Let others see Christ in you and not you in you. "Good and upright is the LORD; / therefore he instructs sinners in the way. / He leads the humble in what is right / and teaches the humble his way" (Psalm 25:8–9).

Grace played hard and led her teams to multiple national titles. But in the end, who she represented took priority over what team she played for. She was proud of her accomplishments but wanted everyone to see God in her. She deflected the glory and let God have it for all to see. You can do the same no matter what you do in life.

Day 44
STRENGTH IN WEAKNESS

Kiara Reinhardt

By Caris Snider

But he said to me, "My grace is sufficient for you, for my power is made perfect in weakness." Therefore I will boast all the more gladly of my weaknesses, so that the power of Christ may rest upon me.

—2 Corinthians 12:9

What would you do if your dream was taken away from you? Kiara Reinhardt endured pain and a long season of unknown after a phenomenal start as a true freshman at Creighton University. Playing college volleyball was all she ever wanted to do, until it wasn't an option.

The Bluejay uniform soared in the air during her 2020 season. As a freshman, she started every match as a middle blocker with an average of 2.14 blocks per game. Kiara's career best came against Marquette with eleven blocks and eight kills. The season ended with her earning a spot on the All-Big East Tournament Team.

All the accolades and accomplishments could not prevent a back injury preseason in her sophomore year. An L5 stress fracture sidelined her for the season.

Kiara had always led with a ball in her hands. Her lifestyle was turned upside down when she was not allowed to move and do the work she trained for. How could she be the person she had always been without doing what she had always done?

Kiara wrote a blog post for *The Fam* about how this injury took her through a dark place: "This injury brought inner struggles and questioning of who I really was. I used to be so sure of myself. I was confident. I was a leader. I was direct and didn't care what others thought of me. I thought my identity was in Christ. These beliefs were quickly flipped. I soon felt timid, confused, weak, and far from God. Everything that had once felt so secure turned to chaos and anxiety. I couldn't possibly understand why God was having me go through this mess of a season. I didn't know how to bring God glory if I wasn't playing volleyball. I felt out of control and disconnected from the only life I had ever known. I slipped into depression and wanted more than anything to be alone."

Do you find yourself crawling through those same types of inner struggles and doubts?

Kiara did not give up.

The weaknesses she had to work through led her to a new anthem to live her life. God would get the glory through her weakness. It would be His strength and not Kiara's getting her back out on the court.

She found her way back into a blocking rhythm with the Bluejay jersey flying high over the net. Creighton volleyball continues in growing a successful program with Kiara on the team. Her key blocks and serves helped the Bluejays defeat the back-to-back National Champion Texas team in 2024 to advance to the Elite Eight.

> *For the sake of Christ, then, I am content with weaknesses, insults, hardships, persecutions, and calamities. For when I am weak, then I am strong.*
>
> —2 Corinthians 12:10

Put in the Work

Kiara acknowledged that the athletes who came before her and opened up about their struggles helped her face the weaknesses in her life outside of isolation. The good news of not being alone in having weaknesses freed Kiara and allowed her to experience God's strength and faithfulness in the midst of her injury. Are you hiding in isolation? Have you come to the conclusion that your weaknesses are too messy for God's strength to shine through?

Get in the Match

Paul is vocal about his weaknesses and the thorn in his flesh. He acknowledges the weaknesses in his life so the God of all comforts can comfort and use him to comfort others. You are not alone in your weaknesses. We all have them. Here are some ways to stay out of isolation when weaknesses are revealed.

1. Stop doing it alone. Pride and fear cause us to take uncharacteristic actions. The pressure you put on yourself because you *should* be able to do it all alone is heavy. The dread of others finding out your weaknesses is paralyzing because once everyone knows "who you really are," they will leave. These are lies the enemy uses on all of us. God doesn't expect you to figure this out alone. Remove this unrealistic expectation off of yourself. "If I must boast, I will boast of the things that show my weakness" (2 Corinthians 11:30).

2. Counseling. Kiara Reinhardt finds counseling to be a game changer in her process of working through her injury. It helped her in the mental battle waging war on her life. Talking to a counselor or a therapist is not a sin. Many of us have found freedom through speaking with someone in this profession. Consider talking to a Christian counselor. They are there to listen and guide you through the internal healing God will reveal as you open up and let it all out. You don't have to keep it close to the vest any longer.

3. Open the blinds. The athletes who shared before Kiara gave an example she could follow. Their stories validated the difficulty in the struggle she faced. Shame no longer held her in darkness thinking she was doing something wrong for being weak. We *are* in fact weak. Open the blinds to your hardships, insults, calamities, and persecution. Share with like-minded believers. Experience God's strength together.

4. Gratitude. An attitude of thankfulness seems to fill so many of these stories. It appears searching for the

DAY 44: STRENGTH IN WEAKNESS

good in the midst of the bad guides all of these fierce females. Kiara expresses how gratitude kept her from going backward in her thoughts as she recovered to get back in front of the net. This one simple practice can change everything in your thoughts and actions. What can you find to be grateful for today? "And let the peace of Christ rule in your hearts, to which indeed you were called in one body. And be thankful" (Colossians 3:15).

5. Get a new anthem. It is always fun discovering the fight song of female athletes. They use this song during the hard practices and the drives to the big games. King David expressed his gratitude when God pulled him out of the pit and rescued him from his enemies, giving him a new song to sing. It is time you found a new anthem to sing as God strengthens you in your weakness. Find a scripture, hymn, or worship song you can keep in front of your eyes and ears to continue forward. "He put a new song in my mouth, / a song of praise to our God. / Many will see and fear, / and put their trust in the Lord" (Psalm 40:3).

We are a limited people with a limitless God on our side. He is not asking you to fulfill His role. He is inviting you to acknowledge you can't.

Day 45

YOU ARE LOVED, REGARDLESS

Jayda Coleman

By Del Duduit

But God shows his love for us in that while we were still sinners, Christ died for us.

Romans 5:8

Jayda Coleman didn't have the best day at the plate—until a teammate prayed. Until Jayda was ready. Until it mattered.

The four-time Women's College World Series champion stepped to the plate in the bottom of the eighth inning with a trip to the WCWS on the line. The Sooners were tied 5-5 with Florida and struggled to get back in the game. The team needed a big play, and Coleman's day at the plate was not her best. On that day, she was one for three with a bunt single and a walk after she struck out and popped up earlier in the game.

A victory over the Gators meant a trip to the WCWS for a

fourth time. Before Coleman made her way to the plate, teammate Alyssa Brito put her hand on Coleman's shoulder and prayed with the team leader. Brito could sense that Coleman needed to calm herself and perform like everyone knew she could.

According to an article in *Sports Illustrated*, Brito approached Coleman and slowed her down and prayed over her. "She was like, 'Surrender it all. Don't try to control everything. Go for it. No matter what, I'm not justified by whatever the at-bat is,'" Coleman said about her teammate's prayer.

On a 2-1 count, Coleman blasted the next pitch for an opposite-field homer over the left-field fence to send the Sooners back to the big show.

"Even though I hit a home run, Jesus still loves me," Coleman continued. "If I would have struck out, Jesus loves me, regardless. I think that put me into my foundation. It's awesome."

It was a moment that just topped off one of the most decorated careers in the history of the sport at Oklahoma. She went from Gatorade National Player of the Year as an OU signee to a multiple WCWS hero. The two-time WCWS All-Tournament Team member, three-time First Team All-American and Big 12 Player of the Year was loved.

God didn't send His Son to die on the cross because Jayda was named to the All-Big 12 Freshman Team in 2021. The Lord did that because she is loved—regardless.

> *For God so loved the world, that he gave his only Son, that whoever believes in him should not perish but have eternal life.*
>
> —John 3:16

Put in the Work

Are you enough? Are you loved without conditions? Do others show you unconditional love? Do you feel you are enough for others or God? No matter what you've done, you must realize that you are enough for the Lord. Some others may not see your value, but always understand that Christ loves you. You are loved if . . .

- You are an honest person.
- You sin.
- You volunteer.
- You pray.
- You scream.
- You laugh.
- You disobey.
- You do what's right.
- You do what's wrong.

Get it? No matter what you do, you are loved.

Get on the Field

To love like Jesus is easy to say. But it's difficult to show love to those you may not like. How do you show unconditional love to someone? It's easy to show that for your family and some selected friends. But what about a person who was released from prison and shows up at your church? Or how about a new neighbor who looks shifty and has an unsavory past? How can you love them? Would you want to be loved? Here are some ways you can show love in a perfect way.

1. Giving without expecting something in return. Never give your time or anything of value with an expecta-

tion of reciprocity. Give to help or just because you love someone. "For where your treasure is, there will your heart be also (Luke 12:34).

2. Listen and don't interrupt. This can be powerful. When you lend an ear without trying to top the story, that is the sign of a true friend and someone who loves the Lord. "Incline your ear, and hear the words of the wise, / and apply your heart to my knowledge" (Proverbs 22:17).

3. Show kindness and patience. It doesn't take a lot of effort to smile, but it might be a struggle to show kindness to those who may not show it back.

4. Forgive instead of punishing. If you punish someone, then you harbor bitterness and resentment. No one on earth is protected from sin. Forgive your family and friends of the sin they have committed. Life is too short to be unforgiving. "Whoever covers an offense seeks love, / but he who repeats a matter separates close friends" (Proverbs 17:9).

5. Speak to others without condemnation. Never forget that you are made in the likeness of Christ. But the difference is you are not perfect. Never look down on someone who is less fortunate and struggles. Speak to them as if they are just like you because they are.

Jayda smacked a home run in the bottom of the eighth inning and helped her team go on to the WCWS. She never gave up on her passion and appreciated the prayer from her teammate. Will God help you send the ball over the fence when it counts in your life? That's not the attitude to have when you pray. Ask God to give you the courage to do what is right. Love others, regardless.

Day 46
STANDING UP BY SITTING OUT

Jaelene Daniels

By Caris Snider

But just as we have been approved by God to be entrusted with the gospel, so we speak, not to please man, but to please God who tests our hearts.

—1 Thessalonians 2:4

Lying in a hospital bed, Jaelene Daniels prayed to God, "Lord, I know I've just been one foot in and one foot out with you, but if you help me out of this situation, I'll find out what it means to fully pursue you."

Chronic pain in her left leg led to the discovery of a blood clot that had formed in her calf muscle and traveled up to her groin while she was a junior at Texas Tech University. The doctor did not mince words and told Jaelene that the odds of her being able to play soccer again were not on her side. Her plea to God paved the way to a miracle.

She had no idea where this prayer of faith would lead her years later as a professional soccer player.

Jaelene spent seven seasons in the National Women's Soccer League with the Western New York Flash who eventually became the North Carolina Courage. She helped lead the Courage to two NWSL championships.

Playing the defender position on the field led to situations where she would need to defend her faith.

In 2017, Jaelene Daniels was extended an invitation to the national team's camp with the opportunity to play a couple of friendly games. Excitement was quelled as she was faced with a decision to make about convictions involving her faith.

The team announced they would be wearing gay pride jerseys. This clashed with Jaelene's beliefs. She met with the chaplain of the Courage seeking wisdom on what to do. Her next step was to gather with those she knew would fast and pray alongside her to know what God would have her do. After three days, she knew the direction in which the Holy Spirit was leading her. She made the call to the coach and declined to play. The news spread throughout the soccer world leading to loud criticism and hurtful noise. She was not prepared for the backlash to come for standing by a conviction God had given her.

Jaelene shared this experience with the students at Liberty University. "It was a day-by-day process with the Lord of asking how I would get through this. It was a decision that I felt He led me to, and in that decision-making, I kept being brought back to the hospital bed and that prayer that I prayed. His Spirit kept leading me back to that moment and saying, 'I'm here with you, and this is what it looks like to follow Me. You're not alone.' That really was my anchor through those few months of just noise."

She would be faced with the same situation five years later and continued to stick by the convictions she believed were from the Lord. She never used her actions or words in a way to be condescending to a group of people nor to hurt. It was important to Jaelene to follow the direction God was leading her no matter the cost.

> *For what will it profit a man if he gains the whole world and forfeits his soul? Or what shall a man give in return for his soul?*
>
> —Matthew 16:26

Put in the Work

Jaelene Daniels was sidelined for staying true to the convictions God had revealed to her. Her choice to be unashamed in her faith was not deterred by potential results. No matter what, she was going to stay all in with Jesus. Are you in the midst of needing to make a decision to stand fast in what God is asking you to do or not do? Does the thought of the world publicly ridiculing you and judging you bring a pause to your steps?

Get on the Pitch

I have to say this was not easy to write. Sharing about personal convictions and how to stand up for those can cause friction. I believe one thing we can learn from Jaelene is to stay true to the creed God has written in each of our hearts and minds. We cannot live to please Him and this world. Here are five biblical examples of those who stood for their faith.

1. Daniel. King Darius chose Daniel to be an administrator and help protect the king's interests. He had a great ability and character. The other administrators were jealous. They schemed together and convinced King Darius to set a law for thirty days. No one was allowed to pray to anyone except the king. Daniel did not budge from his daily prayers. He was arrested and thrown into the lions' den. Not a scratch was found on him the next day. "My God sent his angel and shut the lions' mouths, and they have not harmed me, because I was found blameless before him; and also before you, O king, I have done no harm" (Daniel 6:22).

2. Esther. Esther discovered Haman's plot against the Jews. She knew it was a death sentence to go before the king without being summoned. Esther also knew the massacre waiting to happen if she didn't. God used her boldness to spare the Jews and turned Haman's plot against him. "For if you keep silent at this time, relief and deliverance will rise for the Jews from another place, but you and your father's house will perish. And who knows whether you have not come to the kingdom for such a time as this?" (Esther 4:14).

3. Shadrach, Meshach, and Abednego. These three boys were thrown into the fire because they refused to worship King Nebuchadnezzar's golden image. The fiery furnace revealed four men walking around when the doors were opened. Not a trace of smoke was found on them. Jesus stayed with these young men. "He answered and said, Lo, I see four men loose, walking in the midst

of the fire, and they have no hurt; and the form of the fourth is like the Son of God" (Daniel 3:25 KJV).

4. Noah. Noah started his step of obedience in building a boat when he had never seen rain. He had to make the decision to trust God even when everyone around him was certain he had lost his mind. The ark was completed, the animals came, and the rain began. He followed the lead of God and was spared.

5. Paul. A vast majority of the books Paul wrote for us in the New Testament came while he was in prison. His path started out as a man who killed Christians and even stood and watched as Stephen was stoned to death. He encountered the presence of God on the road to Damascus and was immediately blinded. This moment allowed him to finally see.

Jesus changed Paul forever, and his teachings are what guide us in living out our faith. Standing for your faith won't be easy when the situation arises, but it will always be worth it.

Day 47
GOD WILL HONOR YOUR STANCE

Sage Steele

By Del Duduit

If you were of the world, the world would love you as its own; but because you are not of the world, but I chose you out of the world, therefore the world hates you.

—John 15:19

Sage Steele is not a professional athlete, but for several years she was the face of ESPN and covered the NBA on a regular basis. She hosted *SportsCenter on the Road* from various sporting events such as the Super Bowl and The Masters, and *NBA Countdown* on ESPN and ABC for four years.

Sage was a full-time host of *SportsCenter* and contributed to *ESPN First Take*, *Mike & Mike*, and *SportsNation*. From 2012 to 2020, she covered every NBA finals championship. She was a mainstay in the world of sports—until she went against the grain.

On October 5, 2021, Sage was suspended with pay by the network for remarks she made on Jay Cutler's podcast on September 29 when she shared her opinion on COVID-19 vaccine mandates and how some women dress too provocatively. She was forced to air an apology for her opinions.

Then in April 2022, she filed suit against the network and alleged that ESPN retaliated against her for her views. She said her free speech rights were violated and that the network limited her opportunities because of her comments.

About a year later, the two reached a settlement, and she left the network. Since then, her visibility has skyrocketed, and she has become a vocal advocate for free speech and women's rights. She's teamed up with Riley Gaines and appears on many conversative Christian shows. In an interview with The Washington Stand in August 2023, she said she believes she is where she needs to be with the Lord.

"I feel like God has put me here for a reason," she said. "Not just the way He made me, but ... to get out there and have this conversation and to call out the hypocrisy, because that is what it is. And until someone has the courage to call it out on a larger platform, this will continue. And frankly, there are so many people who are afraid to speak up."

She took on the establishment and did not back down. "I refuse to be quiet about this anymore. I don't care anymore because this is my experience. ... I'm allowed to feel the way I feel. When you try to silence me, I'm done."

> *Do not fear what you are about to suffer. Behold, the devil is about to throw some of you into*

> *prison, that you may be tested, and for ten days*
> *you will have tribulation. Be faithful unto death,*
> *and I will give you the crown of life.*
> —Revelation 2:10

Put in the Work

You may face persecution for your beliefs in life. You may experience backlash for your positions that involve politics or religion. Maybe you will face suspension if you say the wrong words, like Sage did. Perhaps you are a teacher in the public school system and are forced to teach students things you don't agree with on a personal and philosophical level. You may be faced with medical mandates you don't agree with from a spiritual standpoint. Where will you draw the line?

Take the Stance

God made you to be unique. He also gave you a mind and a free will to make decisions. He does not expect you to be a bully and shove your opinions down the throats of others. But He also does not expect you to cower and give in to a different way of thinking. Here are some ways you can take a stand for Christ.

1. Respect authority. It doesn't matter if it's your parents, your pastor, or your boss. You have someone you report to in some way. You may not agree with their leadership style, but God wants you to obey and show respect. Be careful what words you use to describe them and hold your tongue if put in a delicate discussion. Never accept abuse and always set boundaries. "If anyone does not

obey what we say in this letter, take note of that person, and have nothing to do with him, that he may be ashamed" (2 Thessalonians 3:14).

2. Respect yourself. If you need a break from work or from life, then get away for a short time. Take care of yourself mentally and physically. If you find yourself in a tense situation at work or at home, consider some time away in prayer. If you are being mistreated, investigate legal action like Sage did. God looked out for her and rewarded her brave behavior because she did not back down.

3. Respect your peers. There is never justification for making fun of your colleagues or people you associate with. When you show respect, most of the time it is returned. Don't engage in behavior that will compromise your testimony either. "So whatever you wish that others would do to you, do also to them, for this is the Law and the Prophets" (Matthew 7:12).

4. Respect your rights. Set boundaries with workers and family and friends. This is OK to do and will earn respect from those who are like-minded. It will also keep you from sticky situations and from places you do not wish to find yourself in as a Christian.

5. Respect God's will. In all matters of work or play or life in general, follow the will of God. If you find yourself in a unique situation, pray and seek His guidance. Consult with church leaders and with close friends.

Sage drew the line when she was told to apologize for her opinion. She decided to pursue legal action against a company she liked and for a job she loved. God put her in that situation because she would do the right thing and give Him the glory. God gave you courage to demonstrate when the moment presents itself. Stay close to the Lord and stand up for your rights. He will be there for you all the way through.

Day 48

ADOPTED INTO HOPE

Stevey Joy Chapman

By Caris Snider

> *God decided in advance to adopt us into his own family by bringing us to himself through Jesus Christ. This is what he wanted to do, and it gave him great pleasure.*
>
> —Ephesians 1:5 NLT

Stevey Joy Chapman hit the blue mat with the University of Alabama coed cheerleaders in 2025, accomplishing a feat that had not been done for years—winning a national championship. Confetti fell, cheers rang through the crowd, and courage to do high-level stunts was rewarded.

Flying through the air as a college cheerleader was a colossal goal for Stevey.

She was a member of the USA National Team for three years,

bringing home gold in 2023 during the World Cheerleader Championships.

Stevey was adopted from a Chinese orphanage at seven months old. Her parents, Mary Beth and Steven Curtis Chapman, were inspired by their biological daughter, Emily, to begin this adoption journey after a short trip to Haiti. Through prayer and God's leading to help children from China experience love and security, the Chapmans adopted three young girls over time: Shaohannah Hope, Stevey Joy, and Maria.

Adoption has been a blessing for Stevey Joy in the midst of trials and obstacles along her path. While each adoptee's story is different, she sees the beauty in each chapter God is writing in her life.

The Chapmans began their nonprofit, Show Hope, in 2003. In their mission statement, they express that their existence began as a way to care for orphans by engaging the church and reducing barriers to adoption. Show Hope has supported multiple care centers in China for children with acute medical and special needs in the past. Medical care grants and pre/post adoption support is now their focus in helping families feel supported.

Stevey Joy exudes gratitude, reflecting on all God has allowed her to accomplish through her platform presence on social media. She shares this advice she would give her younger self on a video with Show Hope: "I would tell my younger self to trust God, trust His plans for the bigger picture of it all."

Her wise words are a steady reminder for each of us. We can take steps into the unknown knowing His big-picture view is never obstructed. Our hope is secure in Him.

> *We have this as a sure and steadfast anchor of*
> *the soul, a hope that enters into the inner place*

> *behind the curtain, where Jesus has gone as a forerunner on our behalf, having become a high priest forever after the order of Melchizedek.*
> —Hebrews 6:19–20

Put in the Work

As followers of Christ, we are adopted into His Kingdom as sons and daughters. We will look different and be called to unique paths, but His plans for each of us are good. Stevey Joy discovered God's trustworthiness from an orphanage in China to a home in Franklin, Tennessee, to a dorm in Tuscaloosa, Alabama. She did not have all the answers, but she did have all His presence. Are you stuck in answer-finding mode losing hope?

Get on the Mat

Stevey Joy came to terms with not having all the answers. She could still soar in the air toward her goals of cheer with the assurance God would disclose exactly what she needed at the right time. Not having all the answers didn't restrain her from living life to the fullest. Here are five steps to walk in hope while answers are unknown.

1. Fervent prayer. Tests are meant to draw us closer to the Lord. If you experience a desire to linger on your knees, there is a reason. Take this time to be fervent in your prayers. Cry out to the Lord with passion. Go all in on this sweet time talking to Jesus. "Do not be slothful in zeal, be fervent in spirit, serve the Lord" (Romans 12:11).

2. Remind yourself. Remind yourself hope can *never* be lost. Even when all seems lost, living hope remains. In times of doubt, speak out loud to yourself with truth. Tell your flesh God has never lost a battle and He won't start now. "Now may our Lord Jesus Christ himself, and God our Father, who loved us and gave us eternal comfort and good hope through grace, comfort your hearts and establish them in every good work and word" (2 Thessalonians 2:16–17).

3. Remove control from feelings. Your feelings are fickle. In previous days, we have discussed acknowledging our emotions without letting them take control of our actions. Take steps in hope through fact over fiction. Try writing it down like this: I may feel (fill in the blank) but the fact is, God's Word says (fill in the blank).

4. Remember. Look back through circumstances where hope never faltered during extended time in God's Word. Take the extra minutes to seek out another layer of His character and write down what the Holy Spirit discloses. Be still in your thoughts and think on occurrences in your own life where God pulled you from the ashes.

5. Do something. Stevey Joy got active and discovered a passion deep down for cheer. Doubt can be loud and debilitating if you sit in it for too long. Go discover a passion for your life. Attempt a new sport, hobby, or service in your community. Prepare your mind to take action in something new. "So prepare your minds for action and exercise self-control. Put all your hope in

the gracious salvation that will come to you when Jesus Christ is revealed to the world" (1 Peter 1:13 NLT).

Your adoption into God's family gives you nonstop access to His never-ending hope. Now is the time to step out toward your significant goals. Hope will lead the way!

Day 49

GOD IS CONFIDENCE

Zoe Snider

By Del Duduit

And the peace of God, which surpasses all understanding, will guard your hearts and your minds in Christ Jesus.

—Philippians 4:7

Anyone can play basketball, but it takes effort and attitude to be good at the sport. Those two attributes are ones you can control. You can control your outlook on the game and how much work you put into becoming good. You cannot control your height or if you will be born with the body needed to play basketball.

You might find out early in life that the game is not for you and that's OK. But basketball fits Zoe, who is the daughter of coauthor Caris Snider. Although she is good and plays hard for Cullman High School, she has her own personal battles.

"I struggle a lot with my confidence and have had to work through that a lot," she said. "Just life in general. I let stress of all the work I have to do in school and in practice and all my assignments get to me a lot."

Zoe said she will talk about her issues with her friends and family sometimes, but added she likes to go back to the fourth chapter in Philippians and read the seventh verse.

"When I get on the basketball court, I get a little nervous and a little scared," she admitted. "Even though I've put in all the work to prepare and know I'm ready, I still have doubt at times. That's when that verse helps. It makes me feel at peace knowing that God's peace is with me no matter what. Then I feel better. I feel empowered at times."

She also likes to reflect on her admiration for her mother, who has also had bouts with physical affliction and battles with anxiety.

"She's my biggest inspiration and that's legit," Zoe said. "She has cerebral palsy and battled anxiety. She told me stories about how she still did sports and how she worked through that, and that is really inspiring to me. I know I can work through it, too, because of her."

Do you lack confidence? You're not alone. But let's take a look at a few people from biblical days who faced stress. Before David became king, he faced Goliath and was hunted by King Saul. He led armies into battle and dealt with his own son's rebellion. Daniel was in exile in Babylon and defied a decree to worship the king. He was fed to the lions. Queen Esther took a risky step and petitioned the king when she learned of a plan to kill the Jews in her kingdom. She fasted and reached out to her people for prayer. Joseph was sold off into slavery by his brothers and taken to Egypt and wrongly imprisoned for years. He stayed close to God and found comfort.

Those are just a few to remember when you face difficult circumstances. You can have all the knowledge in the world or be blessed with talents and still feel nervous at times. It doesn't mean you are a weak person or weak Christian. It just means you are human.

> *Whoever trusts in his own mind is a fool,*
> *but he who walks in wisdom will be delivered.*
> —Proverbs 28:26

Put in the Work

There are many athletes who get the jitters before a game. It's normal because you want to do well and the fear of the unexpected takes priority. Once you get into the flow of the game, those feelings fade. Former MLB pitcher Orel Hershiser said he used to sing hymns to himself on the mound to calm his nerves. Zoe goes back to her favorite verse.

Get on the Court

How do you handle stress? What do you do to get rid of the anxiety? Do you run or face the music? Do you let the stress and moment consume you or do you find the reason and become a stronger Christian? Here are some ways to handle anxiety and stress and find peace and confidence in Christ.

1. Journal. This is a wonderful way to release stress. When you document what's happening, it can also serve as

inspiration when you go back and see what God delivered you from.

2. Take a break. You can't do this if you are on the basketball court, but you can when your event is over. If you need some time off from work, then take it and unwind. That doesn't make the anxiety go away, but it takes you to a different place for a while where you can recharge and talk to the Lord. "The Lord is my shepherd; I shall not want. / He makes me lie down in green pastures. / He leads me beside still waters. / He restores my soul. / He leads me in paths of righteousness / for his name's sake" (Psalm 23:1–3).

3. Help someone. This will help you see a bigger plan and allow you to examine just how large your problems may or may not be. Perspective is a great tool. "Whoever is generous to the poor lends to the Lord, / and he will repay him for his deed" (Proverbs 19:17).

4. Share. Talk to a friend, a pastor, a counselor, or a group. When you share your burdens, you might be surprised that your issue may not be as rare as you think.

5. Read. Find your go-to verse like Zoe has done and go back to it for inspiration. Some people like comfort food—find your comfort verse.

Stress is part of life. There are enough medications being prescribed for it to prove that. But Zoe finds her peace and confidence in Christ, and you can too.

Day 50

TIME FOR A CHANGE

Merritt Beason

By Caris Snider

> *There is an occasion for everything,*
> *and a time for every activity under heaven:*
> *a time to give birth and a time to die;*
> *a time to plant and a time to uproot.*
> —Ecclesiastes 3:1–2 CSB

Merritt Beason is no stranger to adapting and being flexible throughout her career in volleyball. The right-side attacker has faced change with a growth mindset in every aspect of her life.

The Gardendale, Alabama, native started young in her love for the game. Her dad reflected on their first travel ball match when Merritt was twelve years old. Merritt's team lost in the first set 25-0 with one girl serving the entire time. Defeat opened their eyes to developing every facet of Merritt's skill set.

Her high school years solidified Merritt's dedication to elevating the talent and ability God had given her to an elite level. This commitment to transforming her game paved the way to virtual school. Learning in a new type of environment opened the door of opportunity for Merritt to travel and play in high-level tournaments.

Dedication to this way of life shifted a small-town girl to the big city of Gainesville, Florida. Merritt played her first two years of college volleyball as a Florida Gator, securing her spot on the SEC All-Freshman Team and leading them to an NCAA regional semifinal appearance her sophomore year.

There would be one last change in her collegiate years.

Merritt found herself in a University of Nebraska jersey. Transferring to the red and white renewed her love for a game that meant so much to her. She was treated like family by her teammates, and the value she offered on and off the court quickly revealed itself. Coaches realized the gift she was to their team and named her cocaptain. Players were aware of the gift she was as a human being and dubbed her the mom of the team.

Merritt would go on to help the Cornhuskers make it to the championship game in 2023 against Texas and to the Final Four of 2024 against Penn State.

A new beginning would uproot Merritt one last time. On November 25, 2024, Merritt Beason would be selected as the first overall draft pick by the Atlanta Vibe, finding herself stepping into the pro level.

As God uproots and plants Merritt in new places and stages, her focus is always on sharing His name and Word through volleyball. She had no idea where those beginning pivots would take her. Merritt embraced the God-changes in her life, and He guided her down a path she could not have carved out any better for herself.

> *The LORD says, "I will guide you along the best pathway for your life.*
> *I will advise you and watch over you."*
> Psalm 32:8 NLT

Put in the Work

Embracing change is no easy task. Merritt Beason leaned on her faith knowing God's path would be best. This doesn't mean it would always make sense or be uncomplicated. What change is God beckoning you to make? Is He asking you to become open to doing something new? Is the Holy Spirit guiding you toward steps in a different direction?

Get in the Match

Merritt was determined to bloom everywhere she was planted. Sacrifice and devotion to hard work kept her focused on the multiple reps she needed to take to get her to each stop on her journey. Here are five women who accepted change God brought in their life and how they approached it.

1. Ruth. What would you do after losing your spouse? Ruth chose to follow her mother-in-law and make a change in scenery. She left to go to a land she had never known because she wanted Naomi's God to be her God. She was determined to make this change not knowing what was in front of her. She met Boaz, remarried, and

became the great-grandmother of King David. "But Ruth replied, 'Don't ask me to leave you and turn back. Wherever you go, I will go; wherever you live, I will live. Your people will be my people, and your God will be my God'" (Ruth 1:16 NLT).

2. Sarah. From Sarai to Sarah, God didn't just make a change in her name but in her life. Sarah would become the mother of many nations alongside Abraham, the father of many nations. She was advanced in years, but God delivered on his promise when she gave birth to Isaac. God brought laughter into her life! "Abraham was 100 years old when Isaac was born. And Sarah declared, 'God has brought me laughter. All who hear about this will laugh with me'" (Genesis 21:5–6 NLT).

3. Esther. Esther had to leave her uncle Mordecai and the only home she knew and go to the king's harem. He was on the hunt for a new queen after Vashti had been deposed. Esther was instructed to keep her Jewish identity hidden for a time. When Haman plotted to destroy all the Jews throughout the empire, Esther discovered his scheme and had to go from quiet to bold. Her fierce stance before King Xerxes saved her people and revealed Haman's true character. "When he saw Queen Esther standing there in the inner court, he welcomed her and held out the gold scepter to her. So Esther approached and touched the end of the scepter" (Esther 5:2 NLT).

4. Elizabeth. Barren. Elizabeth was unable to have children. She never wavered in her trust in God. He poured out kindness on Elizabeth and allowed her to conceive and give birth to John the Baptist who paved the way

DAY 50: TIME FOR A CHANGE

for Jesus. What seemed to be a late arrival was actually timed just right. Elizabeth knew her cousin Mary would be giving birth soon after her to the Savior of the world! "You are blessed because you believed that the Lord would do what he said" (Luke 1:45 NLT).

5. Mary. The life of a teenage girl was about to change in the blink of an eye! God sent the angel Gabriel to Nazareth to let Mary know she had found favor with God and would give birth to a son. She was instructed to name him Jesus. Mary did not doubt what God wanted to do in her life. She submitted to this holy shift. "Mary responded, 'I am the Lord's servant. May everything you have said about me come true'" (Luke 1:38 NLT).

Change is a natural part of life. God will use it to catapult you into extraordinary opportunities. How will you respond to His nudge to do something different?

Day 51

IT'S RIGHT IN FRONT OF YOU

Allye Snider

By Del Duduit

I have fought the good fight, I have finished the race, I have kept the faith.

—2 Timothy 4:7

Life is full of choices. Some are good while others may be negative. You will make decisions on where, or if, to attend college. You will have choices to make on what job offer to accept and where to live. Another big selection you will make is who you will spend the rest of your life with and how you will impact the world for Christ.

Some decisions will become routine, like how many cups of coffee to drink each morning and what college team you will cheer to victory.

Allye, who is the daughter of coauthor Caris Snider, faced

choices when she was in junior high, just like all pre-teenage kids. "I was trying to find different things that I like doing," she said. "I tried all different sports but liked volleyball the most. I tried gymnastics, dance, baton, basketball, archery. But volleyball is what I really like the most."

When she discovered the sport, her life plans of becoming a lawyer switched to a professional volleyball player and to play it in college. "I just like everything about volleyball," Allye said. "Playing it and communicating is important. I feel like it's the perfect sport to work as a team and get things done."

She added that she enjoys her role on the team but also takes it upon herself to lend encouragement when a teammate is struggling. Allye also feels obligated to represent her Savior as well.

"It's important for me to be a good witness," she added. "I want to be a good example, and I want to help. Whenever we do our drills and if someone doesn't do what they are supposed to do, I will try to encourage them to do better. I'll tell them they did good but also give them a correction and tell them they can do better and how to do it. I feel that's important, and I get the same from my teammates. We help each other."

Decisions, decisions. Life will present a lot of them to you each day. Will you choose to be a good person and help? How will you treat people you encounter?

Some decisions you can avoid. But there is one choice you will have to make that cannot be ignored.

Will you follow Christ?

> *For God so loved the world, that he gave his only Son, that whoever believes in him should not perish but have eternal life.*
>
> —John 3:16

Put in the Work

If you are a believer in Jesus Christ and have accepted His salvation, then that is the best decision you will ever make. But if you have not made that decision, please consider it because it is a matter of life and death. Maybe you are struggling to find your way and need guidance. Perhaps you deny His existence but keep coming back to never-ending questions.

Get in the Match

If you are ready to live the best life ever and stamp your ticket to heaven, then the choice is easy. But living the Christian life will not be a walk in the park. You will face tough choices, but you will have wonderful peace in your mind and heart. When you decide to follow Christ, a carefree life is not a guarantee, but eternal life and a home in heaven are promises from God. Here is what you need to do to call yourself a Christian.

1. Acknowledge your need of salvation. You need to admit that you are helpless and a sinner and in need of the Savior.

2. Believe in Jesus Christ. You must believe that Christ was born of a virgin and lived a sinless life. He was crucified and died on the cross for your sins and rose again three days later and defeated death, hell, and the grave. "For to this you have been called, because Christ also suffered for you, leaving you an example, so that you might follow in his steps" (1 Peter 2:21).

3. Repent of your sins and ask Him for forgiveness. Confess your sins to God and turn away from that lifestyle

of sin. Will you sin again? Yes, you will, because you are human. But the difference is you can seek His face and ask for help and strength. "If we confess our sins, he is faithful and just to forgive us our sins and to cleanse us from all unrighteousness" (1 John 1:9).

4. Pray and read. The Bible is God's playbook to live the best life. Read His game plan for you every day and talk to Him in prayer often. "I desire then that in every place the men should pray, lifting holy hands without anger or quarreling" (1 Timothy 2:8).

5. Live the life. This means to find a biblically founded church and attend it on a regular basis. If you want to be the best volleyball player, you will attend practice and work hard in the off-season. Apply those same rules to being a Christian. Go to the house of God as often as you can and find a small group to support you in your journey.

Allye made the decision to play volleyball after she tried many other options. Don't wait too long and try the things of this earth before you make the decision to accept and follow Christ. The choice is right in front of you. It's a no-brainer.

Day 52

TO KNOW CHRIST AND MAKE HIM KNOWN

Izzy Nix

By Caris Snider

But I do not account my life of any value nor as precious to myself, if only I may finish my course and the ministry that I received from the Lord Jesus, to testify to the gospel of the grace of God.
—Acts 20:24

Izzy Nix and her husband, Bo, make it their mission to know Christ more every day and make Him known wherever God leads them. It took time for Izzy to come to this revelation.

She was a competitive gymnast for most of her life. Morning practice, school, afternoons back in the gym, sleep, and repeat was the only schedule she knew. By her junior year of high school, it all came to a halt.

The wins were no longer fulfilling. Medals and trophies

stopped being fun to pursue. Burnout had taken over her mind and body.

Izzy had come to know Christ as her Savior as a child, but she began to long for more in her life than being identified as a gymnast. She was being pulled into something deeper.

On the *Honey for Your Heart* podcast with Bryson Kessler, Izzy shares a life-changing question one of her coaches asked her as she was trying to flesh out what she was supposed to do: "Pretend like I didn't know you. Who would you tell me you are? How would you answer?"

Izzy paused in a perplexed moment of thought. Her answer began with being a gymnast and all she had accomplished. Her coach gently followed up with this question, which shifted everything: "Do you want people to know you as a gymnast before they know you are the daughter of the King?"

Izzy knew it was time to put down the leotard and place her identity in who Christ is over what she could achieve. Freedom filled her life as she opened her Bible and chased after Jesus.

Auburn was the only college Izzy had on her radar. After some time there, she had the opportunity to put on a new uniform. She cheered for the Auburn Tigers and during this time, met her husband over a blind date.

God has continued to open doors to places Izzy never anticipated going. When Bo went to Oregon to finish out his college eligibility as quarterback, she found herself there after finishing her degree at Auburn. Eugene was a different type of scene than she had ever experienced, but God had divine appointments in place for her to meet people and shine a light for them to meet Jesus.

Izzy continues to live her life in this way in Colorado, cheering

Bo on as the current quarterback for the Denver Broncos. Wherever the Lord leads her, she knows it is for a bigger purpose than football. Izzy understands God's assignment: to know Christ and to make Him known.

> *And when they had prayed, the place in which*
> *they were gathered together was shaken, and they*
> *were all filled with the Holy Spirit and continued*
> *to speak the word of God with boldness.*
>
> Acts 4:31

Put in the Work

You are ready to be FIERCE. God is not looking for the most educated or talented. He only needs your willingness to know Him and make Him known. God will work through your submission to His plan. How will you take steps forward? What obstacles do you need to face?

Get on the Mat

Multiple strategies have been presented throughout these pages to fuel your faith. Day-to-day practical application weaves throughout every story. To a certain degree, numerous struggles were overcome through similar steps. Here are five suggestions to empower your faith.

1. Bible reading. God's Word is overflowing with actions to incorporate in your life and peaceful words when the trials come. Identify a plan you can do daily. Specify which part of the day, time length, and where you will go to spend important moments with Jesus. "I am the

vine; you are the branches. Whoever abides in me and I in him, he it is that bears much fruit, for apart from me you can do nothing" (John 15:5).

2. Prayer. Prayer is our lifeline to the Lord. Kneeling at the altar is not required. Eyes closed and fancy words are not necessary. Crying out to God while driving to work is the right time to pray. Seeking His will for your life first thing in the morning over the opinions of social media is the right time to pray. Talking to Jesus when negative thoughts consume your late-night studies is the right time to pray. You can write your prayers down or say them silently in your soul. Prayer is always right. "Pray without ceasing" (1 Thessalonians 5:17).

3. Arm bearers. Almost every female athlete you read about had someone in her life she could go to in the midst of her toughest challenges. You are not supposed to do life alone. God is not asking you to figure it all out and not use four impactful letters: H E L P. Write down two to three people you can go to who will help carry the heavy load. "Bear one another's burdens, and so fulfill the law of Christ" (Galatians 6:2).

4. Gratitude. God knew the anxieties would be great at times. He made sure to equip us with a simple practice to shift our brains out of this worrisome process. Look for the good around you. Avoid generic groupings and be as specific as possible. Start in the morning while drinking your coffee, and finish your day with thankfulness. Have random moments of gratitude expressed at the dinner table and with your teammates. "Give

thanks in all circumstances; for this is the will of God in Christ Jesus for you" (1 Thessalonians 5:18).

5. Help others. Your skills and talents are not meant just for you. God has gifted you with your abilities in order to reach others. You will encounter someone on the soccer field or behind the desk in desperate need of His love. You will have a teammate in a difficult family situation who will need to know our good Father. You may discover a nonprofit that allows you to do something you love while impacting others who feel voiceless. Look for those hidden actions you can take to serve someone knowing it will never be recognized. Go be the hands and feet of Jesus. "For even the Son of Man came not to be served but to serve, and to give his life as a ransom for many" (Mark 10:45).

The time has come to implement the action steps presented on a regular basis. Fuel your faith and unearth a new level of fierce!

Other books in the Stars of the Faith series

Dugout Devotions: Inspirational Hits from MLB's Best

Dugout Devotions II: More Inspirational Hits from MLB's Best

First Down Devotions: Inspiration from NFL's Best

First Down Devotions II: Inspiration from NFL's Best

Birdies, Bogeys & Blessings: 30 Days of Devotions for the Godly Golfer

Goal Line Devotions: Stories of Faith from NFL's Best

Bengal Believer: 52 Who-Dey-Votions for the Cincinnati Football Faithful

www.ingramcontent.com/pod-product-compliance
Lightning Source LLC
Chambersburg PA
CBHW050553170426
43201CB00011B/1683